THE
ROMANCE
of ELSEWHERE

Remember from Marcelline from my wedding? She is still one of Roger's good friends after being his professor at Cal State.
XXOO—
Julie

THE
ROMANCE
of ELSEWHERE

*A Half-Century of Connecting
By Sea, By Air, By Rail*

Marcelline Krafchick

REGENT PRESS
Berkeley, California

For those who opened doors and windows,
and for
Jennie Krafchick (1868-1972),
who traveled only once,
and that made all the difference.

Copyright © 2007 by Marcelline Krafchick

ISBN 13: 978-1-58790-133-1
ISBN 10: 1-58790-133-1
LCCN: 2007926582

Cover photo taken by the author in Bhaktapur ("City of Devotees"),
Khatmandu Valley, Nepal, in 1997
Book Design & Production by Mark Weiman

Manufactured in the U.S.A.
REGENT PRESS
www.regentpress.net

Contents

Introduction

*If the primary aim of a captain were to preserve his ship,
he would keep it in port forever.*
THOMAS AQUINAS

*Life can only be understood backwards;
but must be lived forwards.*
SØREN KIERKEGAARD

IT WOULD BE MELODRAMATIC to say that stories have stalked me, but they have appeared to seek out my company. A penchant to take more than ordinary risks may have invited drama. But often my behavior had no bearing on events. For example, I spent a quiet afternoon at the American Library in Athens in 1957, reading Whitman's *Leaves of Grass* and James's *Portrait of a Lady*. I can distinctly picture where I sat in the green armchair to the left of the door. The next morning bold headlines announced that a bomb had destroyed the library building the night before.

When this sort of thing keeps happening, it can stir musings of responsibility, a form of paranoia. A more useful course is to pay attention and breathe in the privilege of spanning an intensely rich era. The telling is a celebration of aliveness.

In Henry Miller's novel *The Colossus of Maroussi,* the figure Katzimbalis dazzles dinner and ouzo companions with stories well told but evanescent, unrecorded. My way with stories has been to savor the urgings of listeners to fix them into print. But what was the point of adding my private recreation to the multitudes of bound pages?

In Paris last year, though, the writing began as if I hadn't decided on it, and once begun, vignettes of varying length and mood came spilling out with joyful vividness. But spilling needs an ordering design. My aim was for the mosaic of snapshots to glean a portrait of an era and a single woman traveling through it—within a frame of three modes of travel—sea, air, and rail.

Time had its role, not in a progression of episodes, "and then. . . and then," as if to track a transformative arc. In place of the artifice of plot, playing with a scrambled sequence would focus on portrayal rather than quest.

A career of teaching *The Odyssey* led me to absorb why a journey is the most appealing of story motifs. In shedding the familiar, a traveler meets head-on not only the new and strange but also the reactions to them that routine never triggers. Having to keep their wits about them introduces travelers to their own resources and dimension. In that sense, travel serves somewhat as a muse.

A story can emerge through the act of telling of a story. For forty years I described catching a marlin heavier than myself, in 1960, twenty-five miles off the coast of Mazatlan. I told how the noble creature flashed its iridescence as it sounded freely in the sea, then changed to leaden gray after the crew battered and lashed it to the side of the boat. I would reflect on my remorse at the harvest of reckless hunting. Not long ago a documentary on sea turtles revived the image of the one the crew hooked on our way back to port with the bound-up drab marlin. The impact of the marlin had crowded out the turtle.

When the captain gave me the slain turtle, I invited new friends and neighbors to share it for dinner. I bustled around the mercado for cornmeal, salt and oil, got help in cutting the unyielding flesh, enjoyed support from motel guests when the electric power failed—they arrayed their headlights to face the cooking area. We had an altogether satisfying meal and evening. It took more than four decades to realize, as Sierra Club member and sentimentalist about animals, that while congratulating myself for feeling shame over the marlin, I'd let an inhumane act help define me.

Maybe a well-told tale is as affirming as a well-lived life. The difference between a swirling pre-articulate recollection and one that can entertain both writer and reader is the relishing of form. In the vignettes here I consciously changed nothing but a few names—events happened just as I describe them; often I saved news-clippings, letters, photos and other corroboration, as if I expected one day to be challenged in court. Yet they take shape through that same rhetorical choosing that drives all narrative, whether invented or recalled. For example, a lengthy career and less-than-lengthy marriage acquiesced to the focus of the accounts here.

Up to the 1950s and '60s, more things happened than I could grasp and interpret. But I did remember. I like to think that the stories preserved here profit from that innocence of interpretation at the time. Without means to reflect analytically, I was touched again and again with wonder, and that impact stuck. Waiting, perhaps.

By Sea

IT WAS THE FIRST Atlantic crossing for any of us in an easterly direction. My first sea voyage was a major family to-do; aunts and cousins assembled at the harbor to help my parents and little sister see me off on the *S.S. United States* and to ogle the liner's dazzling public-rooms. The year was 1954. My grandmother, who, with four little ones in tow, had made the westerly crossing a half-century earlier, stayed home on account of bunions. When my father had told her I'd won a Fulbright scholarship for a year in England, she replied, "So? Are you gonna let her go?" Although I'd been financially on my own through college, this voyage was my great chance to be let go.

With such a long absence ahead, it was the family consensus that I needed a steamer-trunk, of the sort one might have seen being wheeled onto the *Titanic*. My wealthiest aunt offered to provide one, under terms so ambiguous as to cause a rift between my father and her for a decade, nearly as long as a later rift over burial plots.

But this trunk was worth a family rupture or two. It was fortified by gleaming brass corners, rivets, and locks with dangling keys suitable for a garrison. A virtual armoire, it held within it a bank of wallpapered drawers, a brass rod with a dozen hangers, and enough space to dispatch a cousin along inside. Though I remember none of the festivities beyond exclamations by reconnoitering relatives, I do recall my coolly concealed jubilation at this severing—this launching toward autonomy.

*   *   *

The return a year later began on a less celebratory note. I'd run out of the Fulbright money and my plan was to board the Cunard liner *Britannic* the night before it sailed from Liverpool. But it turned out that the ship wasn't arriving from Southampton until morning, and I had nowhere to stay. The local YWCA was "full-up," but the staff directed me to an address a few streets away where they assured me I'd be taken care of.

The woman at the door, hearing that I'd been sent, appeared to expect me and ushered me to an office where I was promptly handed a "boiled nightie" and assigned a room, with instructions, "lights out at nine sharp" and "you're to help serve porridge at seven." At nine that night, someone rapped on my door, announced the time, and asked whether I'd removed my undies—as bizarre a welcome as the bars on the windows. But I was weary and grateful for the clean bed.

Serving morning porridge was an agreeable way to

meet the other girls, who were star-struck over my nation-
ality—"Do you know Betty Grable?" This inter-cultural
pleasantry was interrupted, though, by an attendant tapping
my shoulder and beckoning me to the warden's office. The
warden, a plain fiftyish woman commanding a plain desk,
explained the place I'd come to.

"Magistrates," she said, "direct wayward young women
from the streets to this facility to begin a more correct life."
She must have seen me wince at the word "wayward" and
proceeded to apologize for the misunderstanding made
evident by the discovery of my U.S. passport, an artifact
that apparently disqualified me as a hooker working the Liverpool streets. Handing it across the desk, she began a pitch
for donations and counted out three fund-raising brochures
to take home to friends and family.

*   *   *

The noble trunk having been sent ahead, the next day's
departure on the *Britannic*—this was late August, 1955—
brought a crisis of how to get money to tip the stewards,
whose livelihood depends heavily on gratuities. The answer
was Bingo, with free entry and generous odds. A loan of ten
dollars parlayed into thirty, at that point in history enough
for both cabin and dining steward. When the *Britannic*
docked in New York, I telephoned a cousin—so much for
autonomy—who found me a place to stay at a friend's. The
next day I found a room on Riverside Drive for eight dollars
a week, with roaches scuttering on the dresser after dark,
and two jobs, one at Columbia half-time with a project
in Afghanistan and the other teaching modeling at John

Robert Powers agency. With Columbia's employee discount I registered to study anthropology with Margaret Mead, and the next chapter had begun.

But there is more to the *Britannic* crossing. Two days out, on my birthday, we were descended on by Hurricane Hazel, one of the three most massive storms recorded in the Atlantic. While the 35,000-ton vessel lurched wildly, we heard trays, pots, and dishes flying and crashing in the kitchen. Max Eckstein, a fellow literature student, and I bundled up well, climbed the stairs and forced open a door to make our foray into the deafening storm. Hawsers the girth of a man's arm were fixed along the railings, and we clung to them to spy over the side. What we saw astonished us. The screws under the ship became visible with the sea's monstrous sucking away from it. Pummeled and tossed, we'd imagined the sea colliding with us, but instead it was vacuuming support from under us. In a minute a crew member in wet yellow slicker and fierce expression approached, shouting and gesturing to go below-deck, and we scurried down like the pair of guilty brats we were.

Thirty-seven years after Hazel, at a Manhattan birthday party, I saw Max again, a professor at Queens, and asked if we really did see the screws under the ship. "Of course" was his golden assurance. I turn to this story whenever I feel a craving for credibility and remind myself that it sometimes takes a while to happen.

*   *   *

The hurt and accusation in Mr. Bekiaris's eyes will not fade away. He'd trusted me, and I didn't have the civility to explain why I left. He's long dead now, it won't hurt anyone to tell the story, and it may exorcise that look of disappointment forty-five years ago.

Dorothy Dutcher, who according to rumor has met her maker as well, had been a college chum a year ahead of me. Dorothy wrote from Athens that she had a choice teaching job and would find me one if I'd sail over—this was before jet planes. I wrote that I could scrape together only one-way passage, but she insisted she'd put me up until I got on my feet.

It quickly became clear that a job in Athens would not be easy to find, either teaching at Dorothy's school or elsewhere, for an English-only speaker, and tension grew between us when I turned out to be no longer the wide-eyed junior admiring the sophisticated senior, but someone who spoke up and could disagree.

My major offense came when a suitor of Dorothy's, a candidate for Congress, flew over to Greece mid-campaign to woo her, and while she hid listening behind the armoire, she sent me to greet him at the door with excuses. The fellow, weary from a murderous propeller-flight and distraught that she was out, couldn't find his way to say goodbye. He lingered at the door while she gestured frenetically for me not to let him come in and sit. Slouching against the door frame, he spun out his sad tale, while I saw her bent over with silent guffaws. At last he gave up and accepted that I had no idea when she'd be back.

"Good job," Dorothy lauded.

"Cruel and cowardly" was my assessment. The next day Dorothy told me a home-town friend was coming to stay and I'd have to find lodging elsewhere.

With no return ticket or means of income, I was not amused by Dorothy's parody of generosity as she helped me with my suitcase down to the Athens YWCA. I had enough drachmas to pay for two days of job-searching, and then—what? I was on my own, my father pained to part with "one red cent" for my frivolity and friends at home little more affluent than I.

At the Embassy, U.S.-based businesses, airlines, and newspapers, it was all futile—there were so many like me. The second afternoon, as I walked home from the last pair of shrugged shoulders and hands spread in the air, I felt in the bottom of a pit—no connections or resources, no place to stay after this night, loathing my former schoolmate, and myself for lack of prudence, friendless on the Continent. More even than alienated, I felt frightened and fraught with questions as people bustled around me on the street. Where will I be tomorrow? What will I be doing? How will I survive? And so on. Then I caught a scrap of memory of Thomas Carlyle's *Sartor Resartus* and how he told of progressing out of this kind of abyss. What I remembered best was, "Do the duty which is next at hand."

Involuntarily, I simply cleared. Whatever I'll be doing tomorrow, I'll be doing something. Wherever I'll be, I'll be someplace. Meanwhile, I'll take advantage of the shower at the Y and wash my hair. Circumstances were the same from one minute to the next, but I wasn't. The challenge to be brave translated into a celebration of consciousness.

I walked back to the Y, sure at least to have clean hair and underwear when I checked out the next day.

The cork bulletin board on the hallway wall had been empty, but tonight there was a new white card held in place by four thumbtacks. "Wanted: English speaking young woman, English or Irish, to offer conversation two hours a day in exchange for room and board." My heart did a somersault. Before I could think, I phoned the number. A gentleman explained that Americans were not included in the offer, only British, but in my best English tones I persuaded him to audition me, took a trolley out to Plateia Amerikis, where the Bekiarises lived in a fashionable condo, and landed the job.

They were newlyweds and an odd match. He, Alexis, educated, from an old distinguished family, a collector of fine leather-bound gilt-lettered books, had been a bachelor till fifty-five. She was a buxom, large-toothed, thick-waisted island woman who admitted to thirty-five. I think both did something to darken their hair. My memory has blocked out her first name, but I see and hear her as if it were yesterday. Her voice could cut glass, and she had a way of shrieking "Alekko" that rang through the nine rooms of the elegant apartment, formerly his bachelor pad.

He was truly smitten, and gratified that his playmate had found a suitable playmate. He took us out to dinner a few times, but generally the agreement was for breakfast and dinners at home, served by the maid from Smyrna, Turkey, whose name I recall with ease, Kalliope, a woman whose sallow face looked as if it were in the process of melting down toward the end of her nose.

The routine went this way: whenever Mrs. Bekiaris would rise, our two hours of conversation would commence, with her patting the edge of the bed for me to sit. That could be as late as eleven. But she suspended the clock whenever, still in bed with her breakfast tray, she engaged in long phone conversations punctuated with riffs of shrill laughter. I would go into the kitchen during these periods and help Kalliope cull out the defective lentils. When the lady of the house was done with each call, some lasting up to an hour, she would shout that the English time was resuming. In this manner I didn't get to enjoy free time until two or three in the afternoon. Still, I was grateful.

In the evenings, the unofficial routine was that Mr. Bekiaris, between pleasured slurps of lentil soup, would ask, "And how did you lovely ladies enjoy your day?" Mrs. Bekiaris would show off her progress in English by describing which squares and streets we had strolled or shopped in. He always looked paternally pleased, and turned to me to fill in. His own English was impeccable—he was an industrial executive and had traveled. He sometimes told stories of his own. Once, he said, shortly after their marriage last year, he came home to find her delighted that she'd sold all his books to a peddler—by the pound. When I responded, aghast, "By the pound!" he patiently described his philosophy that in youth one leaps upon and seizes information from books as a tiger, but in later years becomes like a python, digesting continuously, with no more need to pounce. She tried to follow while I tried to fathom this nice man's rationalization.

So all three of us were pleased, as my progress in Greek manifested in longer conversations with the cook Kalliope, who thought it decadently American to wash tomatoes. I was also getting more students for thirty drachmas, one dollar, an hour for conversation in their homes or in the park. Arrangements were not easy, as most people didn't have phones. My pupils were normally scientists with some command of English who were about to attend an international conference and wanted to brush up on their skills. Before long I almost had the $175 fare home across the Atlantic.

One sunny afternoon, Mrs. Bekiaris took my arm and walked me over to a park some distance from home, then instructed me to wait exactly at the bench where she was to leave me for a few minutes. I watched as she bounded like a carefree child across the length of the square to a waiting grey sedan and jumped in when the door was flung open by the arm of a dark-suited man.

I waited. The breeze stirred the leaves across the ground. I waited. Shadows of nearby buildings crept slowly across the square. I waited.

At dusk the grey car returned, stopping closer, so I could see the man, as Mrs. Bekiaris wriggled out and came over to me. Her lipstick was smeared, her hair disheveled, her blouse partly unbuttoned. She said not a word as we walked swiftly homeward.

That night the suddenly-dreaded question came during the soup course. "And what did you lovely ladies do this afternoon?"

She sprang to answer, waxing voluble. "Oh, Alekko, we walked through the markets and looked at all kinds of fabrics and almost bought some, and we watched children in the park." Again, he looked benignly upon her facility with English, while I detested her facility in deceiving him. He turned to me at the same time she did, both looking for elaboration. I gave none, busy with my food.

When we were alone the next day, I gave her notice. I had heard about a basement room with a window onto the passing legs of people and donkeys, for nineteen dollars a month including morning coffee. I told Mrs. Bekiaris merely that I had decided to move. She shrieked as if I'd stabbed her and, whirling in one direction and then the other, began heaping scorn on me for ingratitude. I went to my room and packed. But among her hysterical phone calls was one to her husband's office. He was so distressed at both the news and her reaction that he hurried home.

I was about to reach the door with my suitcase when he arrived. The two of them, side by side, his hand on her shoulder, confronted me. She vented charges of betrayal—ironic in view of her shrewd reading that I would not expose her—and he spoke of his profound disappointment in my character and the injury to his beloved. Knowing I would soon be out of their existence, I offered mild apologies and no defense.

But I'll always remember the mixture in his eyes of hurt and bewilderment. And I can imagine their conversations at the next few dinner meals, perhaps a little in English, for practice, as he comforted her for the cruel outrage she'd suffered.

*   *   *

Many acts of kindness have come from people I never saw again and whose names I can't retrieve. One benefactor I remember only for her red hair and her distinctly generous offer. She lived across the corridor at Clifton Hill House, Bristol University's dormitory for women, and our usual conversation was about the odor of food coming through the floorboards from the kitchen below, especially on Sunday mornings, when they served kippers, a smoked and salted herring, along with baked beans on fried bread, bread so hard that when cut it often flew halfway across the room. We also joked about the cold weather, and I told her how grateful I was that students were required to wear our long black academic robes over our clothing in unheated classrooms.

One week an announcement circulated that the University would be conducting a lottery to choose twenty-six of the twenty-six hundred students to attend a reception with the Chancellor, Sir Winston Churchill. The excitement was palpable and we all applied. When the results were published, and my neighbor had won, she knocked on my door and offered me her ticket. She said, "I might have another opportunity in my lifetime to see Sir Winston, but you're not likely to." And so because of this kindness I got to talk with him. But I was so awestruck that I retained no fragment of our conversation. It was like having a chat with Lincoln.

It was likely that he asked about my course of study and I told him I hoped to be the great American dramatist. That's what happened with a plain-looking grey-haired woman at a reception at Fishmonger's Hall when we Fulbrights arrived. She had an overbite and no style at all in hair or gown, but she was sweet and generous in her interest, so I waxed forth on my dreams. When I moved on to younger and prettier people, my friend Liz from the University of Mississippi sprinted over to me and asked, "What did she say? What did she say?" I told her that I'd done the talking.

"Oh, no, didn't you know that was Eudora Welty?"

After the reception I had supper with a handsome young poet who was brave enough to stand in for the announced guest, a no-show, T. S. Eliot. As with the conversation with Churchill, I wasn't functioning as a thinker—that development would take several years yet. But I remember his name, William S. Merwin.

*   *   *

Tom Skidmore, studying at Oxford, invited me to take part in a political campaign of a British friend of his, and so arrangements were made for us to ride through many streets in a loudspeaker truck. I didn't quite realize the significance of the campaign until after our candidate won. He was Anthony Wedgwood Benn, son of a viscount, who had decided to relinquish his inherited seat in Parliament's House of Lords to run for the House of Commons. For decades I watched left-wing Tony Benn's career with admiration and an unwarranted tinge of pride.

*   *   *

Clifton Hill House was simply too cold to remain the winter of 1954-5. I found a pleasant room near the University on Victoria Square—pleasant in that its neatly curtained windows looked out onto a park, but all efforts to take the deep chill out of the room proved futile. The small gas heater on the hearth of the defunct fireplace devoured shillings, but after I sat ten minutes up close to it, my shins were nearly seared but my calves were as cold as ever. Long before electric blankets, I had to iron the sheets before I could get into bed.

The landlords, Mr. and Mrs. Turner, were a grey narrow couple with the quaint habit of referring to each other by last name. She once mentioned it was offensive to presume possession, as in "my husband." The one memorable feature in this pale couple was Mr. Turner's hair, slicked forward to an "S" swirl on his forehead. The Turners normally did not appear together—one or the other would lurk in the lower corridor or the front garden.

I learned British English from the Turners. Men were not permitted upstairs, where three ladies lived, and when my beau Tony Carpenter from Rhodesia was to collect me for a formal ball at the University, Mrs. Turner brightly offered that Mr. Turner would be glad to knock me up. After they met Tony and he came to fetch me a second time, the Turners allowed that Tony might knock me up himself.

My next-door neighbor was a frail little woman in her fifties with frizzy gray hair who spent very little time out of her digs. Only twice did I meet her on the stairs. Another resident on my floor was an unwelcome one, a mouse, who challenged me to defend my sparse food supply from his brilliant nocturnal raids. I would stuff all apparent spaces and put cheese on a dish in the center of a bowl of water. He found all such measures easy to broach. He even began to steal my stockings, one at a time, left to dry on a rack, maybe to build a nest behind the walls.

One night when Tony and I had been to another grand ball and had drunk rather too much shandy, I collapsed into bed too weary even to remove my earrings. I dropped my gown on the floor and dove under the cold covers. Some time later, in the wee hours, I awoke to the wss-wss-wss of the mouse. Still a bit tipsy, I called out, "Why don't you leave me alone? I wish you'd go back to your wife and children." A bit amused by the little drama, I repeated my lines, adding something about theft of possessions, then fell back on the pillow and slept soundly.

In the morning two things happened. First, I found that all the cheese placed high on a box over another box was gone, along with one more stocking. This was in the days when mending shops for hosiery existed to repair "ladders."

Second, when I dressed and descended the stairs on my way to the greengrocer's, Mr. and Mrs. Turner were standing together in the corridor, between me and the door, their usual smiles replaced by frowns. He spoke for them both, after clearing his throat. "We have certain information, Miss, that you have violated the rules of the house. You must understand that we take these rules very seriously, and we take pride in conducting decent and reputable lodgings. We request that you make plans to leave the premises and find other lodging by the end of the fortnight."

That is how an adept rodent, who, after all, might have been a female, together with a mousy neighbor with not much of a life, managed to evict me.

*   *   *

Now about the greengrocer. Around the corner from my digs was a small produce shop owned by the couple who also owned the busy pub across the way. The shop was normally left unattended, with prices crayoned large on each box and instructions to weigh one's apples, potatoes or onions on the scale on the counter and leave the correct amount next to it. It was a chuckle to participate several times in this ritual of trust, and I told the proprietor so when we finally met. Peg, an energetic woman of about forty with a noticeable limp and a crown of blonde braids, was delighted as well, to learn I was American. She'd fallen hard for a G.I. during the war who was stationed nearby and almost left her husband for him. She still dreamed of him, and her husband knew.

Peg and I became buddies as I learned to cook, with her advice, and she recommended lodgings, a travel agent, and a dressmaker for alterations. One day I had news for her but the shop was empty except for fruit, eggs, vegetables, and a few shillings on the counter. I suddenly realized that with all our sharing of secrets, I'd never told her my name! So I left a note: "Dear Peg, Great news! I've found digs very close by. Your American friend."

The next day as I approached the shop door, Peg hurried out, grabbed me by the arm, and dragged me across the road to the bar of the semi-dark pub. "Here's the friend, Tom, as I told you. She's the one who wrote the note. It wasn't him." She gently pushed me in front of her. "Go ahead, tell him." And I did, and we three became great friends for years after.

*   *   *

In late spring of 1962 I booked passage on a vessel down the Adriatic from Venice to the Athens port of Piraeus to see Spiros and Maria Mavragiannis, friends I'd known during '58-59. It turned out to be lucky I didn't notify them I was coming. There was one stop on that three-day journey, a place I'd never heard of called Dubrovnik, a walled city in the nation of Yugoslavia.

As often happens with student-age travelers, a group on their way to lunch absorbed me into it, introduced me to fried sardines, overwhelmed me with questions about America, and demanded that I spend the summer in their town—they knew plenty of places to stay. I went back on the ship just long enough to throw my things in my suitcase and notify the staff, and returned to spend a summer of culture, relaxation, recent political history, three exquisite meals a day, and true affection with a remarkable family who included me in all their doings.

My room was large. It held a grand piano, draped with a colorful Spanish shawl and always topped by a bowl of fresh fruit. The room was fifty meters from the sea, where I swam and paddled on an air mattress, reading novels, most of the day, except for meals, siesta, and post-siesta rakia (brandy). This afternoon ritual was attended by old friends who shared classical music and survival of the Nazi thugs, the Partisan thugs, and now their current thugs, the Communists, who demanded fifty percent of the rent, which was $5.50 a day, including everything.

During that summer, Sonya, an archetypical earth-mother, recounted stories in perfect English of her child-hood, of local history, of values learned in The War, when only one member at a time could wear the family shoes, and they sustained themselves on potatoes and greens. The teenage daughters, meanwhile, could hardly get over the fact that I was American, and when word arrived that Marilyn Monroe had died, all their friends came to pay respects, weeping and bearing flowers, to "your Marilyn."

This was a magical summer. A friend of Sonya's who had rescued and hidden her two daughters during combat in the city, took me on sailboat rides along the Croatian coast—clearly he would have walked through fire for her. Evenings in the Atrium of the Rector's Palace downtown I heard pianist John Browning and soprano Leontyne Price from front-center seats for sixty cents. And for dancing and laughing there was Max, a Dutch businessman/Egyptologist with a distinctly European moustache, who after he left waited for me at each weekly arrival at Amsterdam. At Sonya's we laughed at his odd ways and his jokes, some of which still amuse me—"Oh, the terrible uncertainty" was making the rounds of the Continent.

I learned how to relax that summer, when Sonya gently pointed out how I turned everything into work, even decisions over how to return home. I adored her parents—the mother a former opera star and the father a former diplomat to the Court of Franz-Josef. He'd owned the first automobile on the Dalmatian coast, and had bought the young Sonya an ermine coat and a pony (I saw the photo, of course). Under the Communist regime their villa had been divided up into eight apartments, one of which they were permitted to rent. It was gripping to pass through the gilt-ceiling halls strung with clothes-lines and smelling of cabbage. Remembering the fifty-percent the Party confiscated, I asked Sonya whether the family felt any bitterness, and her answer was precious to me. "We learned during wars what really matters, family, friends, kindness, music. These gangsters come in succession, the Nazis, the Partisans, the Commies, all the same type—they come and they go—we ignore them and cherish one another." I have material farewell gifts from them, but this gift was primary.

Forty-two years later, after several changes of address and sloppiness about correspondence even with cherished people, I'd lost them entirely and had only Sonya's name. In the era of internet travel searches, a cruise tempted me partly because it would stop for a day in Dubrovnik. Would it be possible to trace them?

After a morning bus tour of Croatia, and prepared not to succeed, I went to the Post Office downtown and grew even more skeptical when I leafed through the Serbo-Croatian directory and found its complex organization baffling. On an impulse I waited for a lull in the line, approached a kindly looking postal clerk and simply asked for her help. I printed the name Matijevich-Wregg on a slip of paper. She took it with curiosity, leafed through her directory, picked up her phone, dialed, and nodded me towards the phone booth one finds in European post offices. When I hesitated, she nodded more eagerly, and I took the phone. And there was Ititza, the teenager now nearing sixty, exclaiming, exclaiming over how they'd talked about me—and Max—and wondered about us. We sputtered and exclaimed, and she asked where I was—I told her I was shortly due back on board. I was no longer a person who would jump ship.

As I feared to hear, Sonya had died a decade before. Ititza said they don't have email, so she carefully spelled out their address, which I wrote on a piece of paper before we professed again our mutual affection.

My cabin steward mislaid that paper. But I'll find the family again. On the other hand, one can overdo closure. Sometimes you can just leave it alone.

*   *   *

In early October of 1957, I was in my Venice bedroom making my bed when the Italian radio broadcast was interrupted by English language in a slight Russian accent. There are moments when one's world turns upside-down in larger ways than personal. The voice announced, it virtually crowed, that the free and most powerful nation in the world had launched a satellite into space that would revolutionize scientific thinking and progress. It was called Sputnik, and it showed the enslaved capitalist nations of the west, chiefly the

arrogant and hypocritical U.S., that the discipline and dedication of the free Soviet Union was superior in education,
research, and vision for the future. It would be months before the U.S. would respond with its Explorer and programs
to enhance science education in the schools. I remember at
that moment, though, being split between defiant jingoism
and susceptibility. What if everything I'd ever heard was just
as slanted one way as this broadcast evidently was the other,
and political truth was more elusive than I'd guessed? That
was the start of a long, questioning political journey.

*   *   *

Here is a case for going places alone. My intuition usually warns me, but one time I ignored it, at some cost.

The *Marco Polo* docking in Buenos Aires for less than
three days, its passengers had much to take in, from architecture to museum to opera house to tango demonstrations.
But one destination I yearned for was Iguassu Falls, which
I'd seen in a Robert deNiro movie called "The Mission."
The Falls are on the border between Brazil and Argentina,
and it would take considerable maneuvering to arrange a
visit.

I found a travel agent in the hotel lobby and spent about
two hours working out a plan and waiting for responses
from his contacts. It was possible to cram a short visit into
the day of New Year's Eve and yet return in time for the big
party. We were scheduled to leave for home the next day.

The plans were elaborate–a limo to the airport, a small
plane, an agent to meet me in a hired car, pick up a local
guide and take me to a boat-station to the Falls for less than

two hours, then back, then a return flight and limo. All in all, it was worth it to me.

As I started to get up from the soft chair, a portly man who'd been lingering around the lobby came over and apologized for having overheard—I recognized him from the ship—and asked if he and his wife could join me and share the expenses. My intuition promptly shouted "No!" but the agent and I heard him out. I asked if he could run or walk very fast if he had to, and he assured us he could, and his wife was athletic. We spent a few minutes more with the agent and learned that I saved barely twenty dollars, because the car for three would have to be replaced by a van for five.

When I saw the wife in the morning walking towards me, I was shaken. This was the insufferable rule-breaking smoker on the ship. In the limo the husband mentioned that he'd had one lung and part of the other removed, but he could stop and wait for us if we had to speed on. At the plane they pushed ahead and took the two seats available next to windows, leaving me and my camera to a center place. Of course, the agent and guide, seeing a gentleman with two ladies, addressed him as the leader for decisions. I was in a jump-seat in back.

And we had to rush to catch the scheduled motor boat. At that point the husband needed to stop and stay behind when we took the boat. The wife smoked ceaselessly and declared a need to seek a place to buy film—an item sold on the ship, at the hotel, and all over Buenos Aires. Time was growing shorter. At last we ran with the guide to the stupendous falls, worth experiencing for the half-hour there. I tried not to spoil my day with self-flagellating. We made it back in time for the party, which was the best I ever attended—tango performances between sumptuous courses. I vowed to honor my intuition and use this episode as a cautionary tale.

*   *   *

We had a scandal in our high school class. Barbara S. got pregnant and had to drop out of school. She promptly married and had her baby and was the only one in our group who didn't fulfill our manifest destiny of going to college. Most of us girls, knowing the frightful consequences of sex, waited till marriage. At the same time, abortion was illegal, and we'd read about the society woman who arranged for her married daughter's abortion because she disliked her son-in-law, and the young woman had died. I harbored a quiet but solid fear.

Sometimes I wonder how I survived my twenty-first year with my life, my virginity, and my general trust of people. My first visit to Athens, on Fulbright funds, could have been more of a life-changing experience than it was. But it was enough.

I met Spiros Mavragiannis at an archaeological site where he worked for the American School of Classical Studies. He approached me with such seriousness in his eyes that I thought he might announce that Achilles had slain Hector. With propriety and grace he pursued me for a week, with strong hints of marriage. Meanwhile, I met John di Rienzi, manager of Rome's Ciampino Airport, who was in Athens to help design a new terminal, and whom I met when I exited a theater and couldn't figure out the direction of my hotel. With hundreds of Greeks milling outside, I picked an

Italian. He invited me to dinner the next evening and, for a week pursued me with propriety and grace.

When my ship was about to embark for Brindisi, my nearsighted eyes made out two handsome men approaching me with bouquets. We got through the embarrassment somehow, but either of them would have been helpful once the ship left. I was immediately taken aside by an officer with mostly gold teeth who informed me that the captain had directed that I stay in his cabin. When he would hear none of my demurring, that I had a fiancé (did he see me with two suitors on the quai?), that I was ill, that I did not wish to go, that I preferred third class, and dug his fingers into my shoulders, I pulled off an Oscar-worthy impression of someone with severe stomach pains, whereupon he stepped back and let me go to my cabin. What I'd learned quickly before his invitation was that there were no other passengers, only crew, on their way to begin the season schedule from Brindisi, at the tail end of rough weather for sea travel. I remembered the bumbling Bristol travel agent who'd got me into this.

Immediately I removed a rope from around some books and tied the handle of the door, which opened outward, to the iron bedstead, wrapping it around and around, glad that I'd brought an orange and some figs and that there was a sink in the cabin, with a glass. I missed the dinner, announced by a sharp rap on the door and general shuffling and shouting at the wooden tables just outside.

Sleep was welcome but interrupted sporadically by the vessel's violent dippings and heavings in the rough sea. I heard running and groaning, and at one point someone opened the door and placed an empty bucket inside. How could he have done that? Impossible! But the act of charity, curiosity, duty or avoidance of later clean-up was enough to let me fall back to sleep.

In the morning I timidly emerged to learn that virtually everyone aboard had become seasick. Having forfeited a large meal, I had benefited from my hunger. I benefited from the storm as well, in never again seeing the captain or his agent, even at the landing formalities. As soon as we docked I hurried off, suitcase in one hand and books re-tied neatly with their rope in the other.

*   *   *

I didn't know Greek at that time, but later on, after a year in Athens with the express purpose of studying Greek culture and language, I was proficient enough to interpret, for what turned out to be thirty drachmas or one dollar an hour. But aside from opening the door to friendships and history, the language offered me the special fun of understanding without looking like someone who does. An example took place on a ship from Trieste to Piraeus.

My seat assignment for all meals was with three forty-ish Greek businessmen. They were quite gallant, and each individually sought me out on deck during the two days to disclose how they were really poets or artists only making a living with business. They didn't seem to know about one another's courting when they came to the table, but increasingly joked in Greek about the American girl. They became crude, close to disgusting, as I asked them to pass the butter or the water carafe. Back on the deck or in the common-rooms they continued to vie for favor when we would arrive in town. With each of them I agreed to meet at the harbor and taxi together to Athens.

At the last meal before we landed, the fellow across from me told a raunchy but hilarious joke. I had just swallowed a spoonful of soup and couldn't control its exploding out of my mouth in a great guffaw. All three of them asked, "Katalaves?" (You understood?) "Malesta" (yes. indeed), I answered, "Ta kataleva ta olla" (I understood it all).

On debarkation we four table-mates went our separate ways, one of us in good spirits.

*   *   *

There were many rewards in learning Greek, including being able to turn on my heels when young men followed in a combination of flirting and jeering, and calling out to them in gutter slang, "Ti thelis, vreh?" (What do you want, buster?) But possibly the most satisfying non-tourist moment came on a local bus in the outskirts of town when I heard a conversation between two housewives. One told the other, "Have you heard? Over in Voulos a woman gave birth to a calf."

*   *   *

Spending Lent with a family in Corinth, I gave up a gradual progression of staples, meat being first on the list, until finally we lived on sesame gruel. So as Easter arrived, our mouths watered as we took turns rotating the lamb on a spit in the earth. But just before midnight everyone, including the badly disabled, carried candles in a procession to the cathedral. In utter silence, the crowd swelled while two priests stood formally at the top of the stairs before a casket. The tension was suffocating. A toothless old woman next to me said, "I pray that Christ will rise this year, so the crops will flourish."

At last it was midnight, and one priest called out, "Christos anastasis!" (Christ is risen). The other followed with "Alithos anastasis!" (Indeed he is risen.) In an instant pandemonium erupted—guns, firecrackers, shouting, whistles, movement in all directions. A broad-smiling man lifted me by the waist and moved me ten feet from where I was standing.

Before long we all turned and paraded back to our streets. It would be another several hours before the lamb was fully cooked, and we stayed up, taking turns at the spit.

*   *   *

In Communist China trains are not classified in the bourgeois manner into first and second class. Their more and less expensive seats are called soft-seat and hard-seat. The equality concept has its limits. When I visited an East European friend who was proud of his Communist system, he pointed out that I would see no soldiers on the streets, no beggars, no signs of squalor. That evening we went to the opera and sat in box seats. When we came out, I noticed a line of ragged beggars reaching out to the music-lovers. I nudged my companion with my elbow. "Look, beggars," I said.

"No," he muttered. "They are only gypsies."

*   *   *

Going to the movies in Venice was an adventure. The film was projected outdoors in an open field with rows of folding chairs set up, a tall wall for projection, and a ground surface of pebbles that made a great noise when stepped on.

Piero and I went to see Lawrence Olivier's film of *Hamlet,* which I'd seen in our high school English class when it first came out in 1948. It's an especially long film for its time, but the evening was too hot to stay indoors and there was a slight breeze at the outdoor cinema.

I got to see a more engaging show than the movie itself. Only a few minutes into the story, Olivier as Hamlet addresses his father's ghost, using his dagger to vow vengeance. As he raised the dagger, the whole audience stood and shouted, "Don't do it!" "Don't kill yourself!" I almost envied their innocence. It was early in the story named for Hamlet to fear he'd do himself in—but I remembered that Julius Caesar dies very early in the play named for him.

How excited the audience was! But more curious than their naiveté about the plot was their certainty that their warning shouts might change the action up on the screen. Cervantes has a theater scene like that in *Don Quixote,* a lark to read, but sensational to experience from its midst.

*   *   *

Ilda was one of the Ca Foscari University students who took lunch with the Zennaro family. Having finished all her coursework and lacking only the dissertation for the "laureo" degree, she earned her living by writing papers for wealthy students. They could afford her labors, and she needed the income. Ilda was brilliant in several languages, and showed me the five-inch-thick thesis she'd written on Jonathan Swift at Oxford.

When she found a regular job teaching English at a trade school, she invited me to sit in on a class.

European custom was for students to stand to answer the teacher's questions. I enjoyed the class's preparedness and willingness to respond, until one crushing moment. A slim young man toward the back of the room wore steel braces on his back and legs, and when his turn came to reply to a question, it was agonizing to see his contorted effort to stand. Finally he did, and his answer was not to Ilda's liking. Her words burned into my brain precisely: "Your mind is wicked and twisted, just like your body."

Fifty years later I still reel at this incomprehensible cruelty. There is no necessary equation of intelligence to sensitivity.

*   *   *

Once I lied splendidly for a brief pay-off. It happened on my third steamer trip from Trieste to Piraeus, off-season with a light passenger load. A rest would be welcome before a visit to beloved but exhausting friends, mountain climbing, and hole-in-the-ground privies. The purser assigned me to a cabin with an English woman named Shirley, whose agenda was to talk me to death—a form of drowning. She stuck to me from meal to meal, deck to deck, fore to aft, effervescing with silly, unanswerable questions, and would not take polite and then bolder hints that I preferred some solitude. She would talk on while I thumbed through unreadable books in the ship's library. When we stopped at Bari and Brindisi she followed me to cathedrals, though I gave her the slip by entering one door and leaving by another. At a confectioner's where I hid and snacked she turned up screaming at the luck of finding me at last, after a twelve-minute separation. I was desperate. Finally I saw my chance.

Shirley came on deck to catch me staring myopically out to sea, and said I looked sad.

"Yes," I told her and paused, "Can I swear you to keep a secret about something?"

"Of course," she answered, and pledged absolute confidentiality, "on my mother's grave" (I never understood what that meant). I told her that doctors had given me a few months to live and required I spend them in complete quiet. It sounded so soap-opera that I waited for her giggle, but she grew teary and—could it be?—quiet. The rest of that day I enjoyed as I'd wished from the first.

That evening the captain sent a message inviting me to join his table for dinner. He treated me like an Onassis at the dinner table and like fragile china on the dance floor, while passengers all around gazed on with tilted heads and looks of pathos—"so young." When I slipped out to the deck, two stewards scrambled to tuck blankets around my chair. I leave Shirley's mother's grave to whatever fate may have befallen it, but those few hours of solitude remain my most hard-earned.

*   *   *

It wouldn't be quite accurate to say that the Gibraltar Safeway is closed once every 300 years, but it closed in celebration of the August 8, 1704 liberation from Spain by British-Dutch forces. My own pressing politics were that I needed a bar of gentle soap because the facial soap aboard the *Rotterdam* stung my eyes, a complaint I heard from a few fellow passengers.

I'd walked a mile along the oddly abandoned streets without finding the familiar "S," when I came across a man in shorts striding along at a business-like pace, and asked directions. He was fairly certain the store would be closed for the holiday. We chatted a while—he's from Dublin, his wife is from Gibraltar, I might find some small Indian shops open—as far as his building, where we exchanged good wishes. When I got to Safeway there wasn't a car in the lot (puzzling sign: "Adult and Child Parking"—?). A note on the door explained the closure due to the "tercentenary"—a word not likely to appear at home.

Following the road back towards the harbor and finding no shops, I was envisioning milking liquid soap dispensers in the ship's public restrooms, when I heard a call from behind me on the hot, empty street. A gentleman in jogging outfit, about fifty, not the one I'd met, was running red-faced towards me, shouting, "Excuse me! Excuse me!" In his hand was a box of Dove soap he held out like an offering—well, it was an offering. "You needed this. My partner sent it." I lost all presence of mind for an expression of thanks, beyond a gasp, clutching my neck, and the words, "I will always remember this as Gibraltar." That gift buoyed me for days through the rudeness of the American passengers.

*   *   *

On the other hand, back in June of 1961 I had fully disgraced myself among Britishers on a voyage—this time the P & O Orient *Himalaya,* sailing from San Francisco to LeHavre—a twenty-one-day voyage passing through the Panama Canal. My second-class stateroom cost $220.

Now, what was the source of my dishonor? I couldn't grasp it for several days.

Somehow I'd been assigned to the table of the Chief Engineer, whose role the maitre d' had declared was the most important on a ship, more so even than the captain's. We were seated with three couples, all British from various colonies like Burma—almost caricatures—a rubber plantation owner, and so on. At the first meal they were pleasant to me, though they sniffed a bit at my credentials. But gradually for the next few gatherings they grew icy, ignoring me conspicuously. As we arrived at lunch the third day I saw that the very nice Chief Radio Engineer was sitting alone at his table, so I excused myself with what I thought a civil explanation, that I thought he might like company at his meal. I was glad for the change.

The atmosphere at dinner that evening was brutal. I was being shunned, punished and I didn't know why. After all, I was holding my peas on the back of my fork. As we walked toward an elevator, I eased over to the meanest of the wives, the one from the rubber plantation, and asked her how I had offended. She explained with impatient hauteur. It was utterly mandatory to be seated when the Chief Engineer arrives at table, she said, and to remain until after he has left.

Ah, so that was it. How simple. All I had to do was think of the Pope. "It's merely manners," she declared, having herself displayed to this uninitiated foreign girl in her twenties a conduct less mannerly than vicious.

I asked to have my table changed and was duly snubbed whenever I passed any of this group on the deck.

But that trip was not without its fun. At each stop along the way through Panama to Trinidad and Barbados we had a few hours ashore, and I always came back with a tale of bizarre happenings or discoveries, so that my second set of table-mates decided they would follow me. That strategy led me to walk in one Woolworth's door and out a rear one, and somehow meet even more solo episodes.

For example, I walked up Trinidad's steep Laventine Hill on a torrid day. At last arriving at the top I came upon a church with other small buildings. When I sat on a bench to rest, a friar emerged to ask if I were there to meet with Bishop Kennedy. "No," I replied, "but I'd be grateful for the honor."

In a few minutes the affable bishop joined me, had lunch served to us, and invited me to the opera that evening—unfortunately after we were to sail at 6 PM. We had a good chat, especially about his cousin the U.S. President, and when I left he asked me to accept his blessing—I didn't know how. So I bowed my head in thanks for all fine serendipity and the wits to escape the Chief Engineer's idolaters and my table-mates for an outing on my own.

*   *   *

Never mind scandals, I once did do serious harm, though not intentionally. It happened on a steamship from Spain to London that I learned had embarked a month earlier out of Dar es Salaam, Tanganyika (now Tanzania). "Never Destroy This Landing Card," the printed letters have ordered each time I've gone through my personal artifacts, since 1959, when I became a form of Typhoid Mary.

Dysentery is no picnic. I'd lost so much weight from it that my pelvic bones protruded. I needed to leave my friends Nina and Klaus in Madrid and their dear family who kept prescribing white rice, and get back to London, where I had a ticket home. I was far too poor for air travel and too ill and weary for a train, so I asked a travel agent when a ship might sail to London. "Twice a year," he replied. "Oh." I was nearly in tears.

"But what luck. One of those two is tomorrow morning!" So I booked passage on the steamer, where I met and danced through the evenings with Robin, the adorable purser who'd camped all over Africa.

A couple of days out, my neck and jaws started to ache. When the pain moved into my ears, I reported to the ship's doctor (Bachelor of Medicine degree). After examining me he suggested I wear a scarf, and "Sister" (the nurse) would give me some penicillin. But the ache worsened so that I could hardly eat, and I returned to his "surgery." Again, the scarf and pills, this time with a diagnosis: I had parotitis. Meanwhile, Robin and I were enjoying long talks on the deck about Africa and dancing in the small ballroom.

As we neared London, a small motor vessel came alongside and deposited a journalist and a photographer from the London press. The reporter said that I'd been described, no doubt by Robin, as a most interesting American, and he wanted to take some photos together with the children in First Class. When we assembled in that section, he kept telling the young ones, "Now get closer to the nice lady."

And they did, at what price I would never know, but I did know about Robin.

In London I went directly to St. Mary's Hospital, where

a doctor instantly diagnosed the mumps. When he heard that the ship's doctor had said "parotitis," another name for mumps, he asked for the ship's name. He said that had that doctor acknowledged the ailment he would have had to hoist an orange quarantine flag and keep the ship offshore for some weeks after more than a month out of Tanganyika. He'd made a choice that would cost him his career. The St. Mary's doctor sent me to London Fever Hospital across town, where I stayed for three weeks, with doctors and nurses closing faucets with their elbows in my solitary room. With National Health paying for my care, I was an ingrate for feeling sullen about food not fit to eat, and only black-black tea to drink, and no fruit, even for a bribe. Three hospital weeks without an orange.

Robin came to visit with flowers, sympathy, and news of the ship doctor's sacking. I never saw my adorable purser again, but got a letter some time later from his hospital bed, describing mumps as feeling as if a tank had rolled over him. We never discussed, and maybe he didn't know, what it can do to males. I just prayed he'd be spared sterility. What had I done?

At St. Mary's it was early September by now, and I yearned to hear the Edinburgh Festival. So I leaned out a window and pleaded with a gardener to find me a radio. He did! But after a moment's elation I learned that it broadcast only two popular stations, with silly game shows and light music. I lay down and closed my eyes, feeling miserable.

Soon I heard a tribute to the composer Irving Berlin, with the song "God Bless America." I wept. I've heard that song in many contexts, hundreds of times. Never before or since have I shed tears because hospitals in America serve orange juice.

From there I stayed at the pub and inn of my friends Peg and Tom Kerslake in Cornwood, near Ivybridge, and while recovering strength I was a busy barmaid, a magnet to customers from far and wide by the droll way I dispensed draft beer and mis-counted shillings and pence for change. Peg introduced me to the Squire of Ivybridge, who ordered a case of whatever I was drinking. Not as adorable as Robin, but dashing in his white scarf and jodhpurs, he zoomed around the countryside with tales of his spy-years in WWII, pointed out his herd of miniature horses—"mares are just like women, they shudder when they surrender"—and invited me to supper in his kitchen. His mother wouldn't come downstairs to dine with a commoner after the Queen had been her guest a fortnight earlier. The house was recorded in the Domesday Book in 1085. And me a barmaid.

*   *   *

The trip down the Amazon from Iquitos, Peru, is far more appealing to me than the more common trip up the wider end from Manaus, Brazil. The Manaus journey is like an ocean cruise, the river being too wide to reveal much sight of land. The Peru journey keeps the banks in view all along the way, so travelers can keep closer watch of the riverside communities. Besides, the narrower waterway makes for smaller vessels holding only two hundred passengers willing to endure cold showers, sliced white bread, and no packaged entertainment. I noticed also that there was no safety drill or fire extinguisher. But we were in less conspicuous danger than the Peruvians we observed. The year I traveled down the Amazon to the Colombia/Brazil borders and back to Iquitos, the water level was the highest it had been in decades, some thought ever. For the homes that were all built on stilts that meant that if the river were to rise an inch higher, they would have to be evacuated back into the jungle.

What we saw as we gently chugged by were whole living quarters of two rooms, open to exposure without privacy from our gaze, except for an occasional bamboo roll-up. At night these dwellings dotting the riverside were all lit by the same size of small flame atop a vat of kerosene. With the sun setting at six, the long nights found the river people entertaining themselves with song and drink. Sometimes we would hear the murmur of two voices and the paddling of an oar, as a boat would glide up near us to sell carved wooden dolphins for a dollar.

But for the most part, they ignored us and went on with their lives, fascinating in their uneventfulness. A couple of villages on relatively solid ground made some income by arranging social events with ship passengers. We would clamber ashore and be led to a thatched-roof round-house, served strong yerba mate tea, its leaves the size of spinach, and taken by hand to participate in a long, repetitive dance, rocking back and forth for an hour to a simple two-step.

Children as young as three were out in little canoes, one or two to a canoe, wielding their oars with casual expertise. This was apparently like going out to the park to play. American tourists who'd brought plastic toy fire trucks and pails and shovels were met not only with wonder at the items but the fact of their uselessness in a place where the surface was water. It became evident that children, adults, dogs, goats, all defecated in the water, as in Kenya they did in the courtyard of the rondavels.

At night the more plucky of us would descend into small boats with a local guide adept in hunting the alligator-like caiman ordering us not to make a sound, reaching down like lightning into a nest in the dark water and chuckling over our fright as he hauled one aboard flopping and banging a mere three feet from our knees.

During the day we would traipse through the jungle, awed, thrilled—we were in the Amazon!—by brilliant parties of parrots and mammoth termite-nests in the trees. We traced tributaries leading to pink-colored dolphins. The lily-fronds large as dining tables looked strong enough for men to walk on—I lifted the corner of one to find it leathery with millions of soft needles beneath—and the general impression of lush ripeness overwhelmed us. One guide forgot to remind us to take water for a trek, but no matter, his machete whacked off a tree-branch that contained water. He showed us the symbiotic relationship between the tree and the ants scurrying inside its bark. The best surprise was not having insects drop onto us. In fact, the non-Hollywood jungle was clean, by virtue of nature's efficient system—for example, termites made skeletons vanish in short order.

Our last stop was at a long-established leprosarium. The sprawling one-story buildings set back from river's edge had no electricity for refrigeration, and the nun who'd lived and worked there for fourteen years proudly explained how she managed. For one thing, to avoid contracting the disease, she said, she wore long hose (an anomaly in the tropic) and bathed when she got home at night. Her mint-green nurse's uniform was newly pressed and spotless. As for the patients, their fingers eroding off their hands like driftwood eaten down by wind and sand, they were not shy about showing their condition and smiled broadly at their circumstance. Many were crafting items of balsa wood, little canoes with paddles, and, again, dolphins, that we bought for gifts.

Canoes waited at the wharf to transfer us to the ship, and Sister greeted us farewell with thanks for our purchases. Meanwhile, villagers, mostly children, crowded watching us from a shelter built above the boarding-place. I was the first to step into a canoe, and, as I stood on the seat to make my way to the end, my head collided with a false floor on the shelter. The collision was so loud that passengers said they heard it like a cannon-shot from the ship, and it alarmed everyone around. To me it felt as if my head were a melon that had cracked open. Having been warned by ophthal-mologists about blows to the head, I went into a panic, with my hands on my cranium, calling out, "My eyes, my eyes!" No one, of course, would know the meaning of the cry or the source of my alarm, but Sister saw someone in trouble and came quickly to the rescue. Probably thinking I was cry-ing "Ice!" and that she might reduce the swelling, she seized someone's T-shirt, dipped it into the excrement-dappled water, and wrung it out over my head.

Back aboard the vessel I managed eventually to get some precious ice from the kitchen to stem the swelling, though it was small comfort and merely increased my violent shiver-ing. Along with no safety drill or fire extinguisher, there was no radio communication from the vessel to land. So I had to pray to my secular gods until our return to Iquitos, where I phoned for an appointment with my retina specialist on arrival home via Miami. And that is when I heard the best news of my life. Dr. McDonald said after the exam that my retina had been so thoroughly welded on after the last crisis that I had nothing to fear and could continue to enjoy adventures to my heart's desire.

*   *   *

Probably the happiest people I knew in Athens in 1958 were a pair of spinster sisters who'd inherited enough to live on their own. As older women, they dressed all in black despite not being widows, but their humor was delightful and even at times ribald. They were cousins of the owner of a Greek restaurant I frequented in Chapel Hill, and like all Greeks I knew, had no limit in hospitality.

They had a cousin, a young man, they were interested in introducing to me, and one afternoon at tea he joined us, a pleasant, ambitious, slightly self-important businessman. He invited me out to dinner the next evening, I accepted, and he picked me up with his car at my apartment.

We drove through Athens to outskirts I hadn't seen before, and arrived at a complex of low buildings where a valet of sorts ran to the gate to meet and direct us. My companion nodded, accepted a key, and drove around to park just outside a door of what resembled a motel. When we entered, what I saw was a double bed, a table for two, set with a basket of bread and a small vase of flowers. Two chairs, no dresser or armoire. With a genial smile he gestured for me to sit. I did, but said I had to leave right away because of a misunderstanding. He looked puzzled. I said the circumstances spoke of something I would not do with him, or anyone. Puzzled again, he said, "But you travel alone. Your parents allow you to go everywhere alone. That must mean that you do these things. All the blonde Swedish girls who come down to Greece are eager to do it."

All I could think to say was, "I'm not Swedish." Then, "Please take me back."

I fixed a chicken and tomato sandwich in the kitchen, and because Kalliope wasn't there, I violated her rule and washed the tomato.

*   *   *

Molly Ivins, the celebrated Texas writer/iconoclast, was sitting to my left at a round dinner table for eight. We were all strangers on the ship, connected only by the political leftism that formed the theme of the cruise, and everyone knew of Molly. The diner to my right leaned across and asked her how her fight with cancer was progressing. The answer brightened us all—she thought she had the monster licked. In relief a couple of others told of close calls and dire warnings that were happily unfulfilled. One woman across the table said her doctor had declared in 1976 that she had six months to live, and this was 2000. Suddenly, one of us asked for a show of hands of cancer survivors. Eight out of eight raised our hands and established an unspoken bond for the rest of the cruise. What are the chances?

*   *   *

On a geomorphological expedition in a gulet, a sailboat uniquely made in Turkey for its Aegean—"Turquoise"—Coast, a dozen of us measured, counted, and explored at stop after stop. A woman doctor from Maine named Sandra, no longer practicing and estranged from her two grown children, was the most energetic among us. She was the first to scramble up precipices and over smooth rock formations.

At one site where Sandra and I were assigned—it was against the rules to be left alone—she disappeared. Unfazed, I poked around in some interesting-looking rubble. All of a sudden I saw a perfect human mask in miniature about four inches high, made of terra cotta or red rock. I scooped it up into a Kleenex, elated over its beauty and condition. Back in my cabin I placed it on the desk and took some photographs from different angles. The romance could not last. My cousin Dick the Philadelphia lawyer had defended an American woman who was detained in a Turkish prison for four months after purchasing an item designated as an antique, therefore off-limits for export. It was out of the question to remove this lovely artifact—I had to leave it in Turkey, where it belonged. But I could enjoy it for a week before I turned it in.

The morning of debarkation Sandra came to borrow something in my cabin and she saw the face I had to leave behind.

"Oh, no," she cried out, "I can get it past customs." I objected on grounds both moral and practical, but she grabbed it, and at customs when we boarded the ferry to Kos, she merely put it in her pocket and walked through. How pleased she is to have it on her shelf at home, she later wrote. I wonder if the loss of her medical practice had something to do with ethical blindness. She was the bravest among us, but I don't admire her.

*   *   *

One day on the gulet expedition, we were looking for centuries-old mooring-rings recorded by earlier explorers. These were slabs of stone about two-feet square wedged into rock walls and hollowed out with a circle to allow ropes and chains to be attached for anchoring. We were anchored ourselves at Knidos, near the uninhabited island of Gemele, supposedly the birthplace of St. Nicholas.

We could hardly believe what we saw—there they were, two mooring-rings. I grabbed my notebook to draw them, then photographed them. Finally we scrambled to report the success to the others, and as the computer operator in the group, I typed up a record and slept very happily that night. Some adventures are very quiet.

* * *

It's my policy to arrive earlier and stay on later than any group, no matter how small, so I have some time alone in the region. I did that on the island of Kos, before ferrying over to Turkey for the expedition down the Aegean. Not very well known among tourists, Kos offers few sites of interest beyond the lovely harbors common to all Greek islands. And in September of 1992 all the islands were stricken with a severe heat wave. The heat was so merciless that I would go down to the harbor and get on any small boat going anywhere, just to have some wind on my face. After two days I packed my bag and took a speedboat over to the justifiably famous Patmos, where I stayed at the idyllic hotel Romeos and practiced my Greek with the owner's family. To say they were hospitable would be redundant—they were Greek.

After two days I took the last possible boat back to Kos

to catch the morning ferry across to Bodrun. Ten minutes or so out at sea, savoring the refreshing breeze, I suddenly realized I hadn't retrieved my passport from the hotel owner. Oh, no! I spoke to the captain, who said it was impossible to turn back and there wasn't another boat till the next day. He radioed the hotel to be sure the passport was there, and it was. What to do? I couldn't get over to the expedition I was committed to (and had paid for) without my passport.

In Kos I consulted the harbor official (Greek, ergo hospitable), who made a suggestion. There was a mail ship that arrived at the island every weekday morning at 3:00. He could radio the Patmos hotel and tell the owner to put the passport on that ship. We arranged that, and I asked my Kos hotel clerk (Greek, ergo hospitable) to wake me at 2:00. The only problem at that point was that the port area harbored not only sea-going vessels but the roughest of characters, usually drunk, ergo too hospitable..

But I had to do it. So at 2:30 I followed the dim yellow lights on poles dotting the horseshoe-shaped Kos harbor, looking constantly over my shoulder. Near the port itself was a taverna where raucous voices spilled into the air. I had to pass it, then waited for the mail boat, not knowing whether to hide in the dark or stay in as much light as possible.

A little after 3:00 the boat eased up to the dock. Its front yawned open like the door of a roadside mailbox, and as soon as it bounced flat, a man scurried past me and came back out with a white pouch, apparently the Kos mail. I ran over and asked the first uniformed fellow inside to look for my passport. He disappeared for a few minutes, then returned saying he'd hunted everywhere it could be, and it wasn't on the vessel. They were getting ready to move on, so

I stood on the dropped door and said in my best Greek, "I'm not leaving this spot until someone finds my passport. Let me talk with the captain."

In a minute the captain walked out of the dark and greeted me politely. I declared (bluffed) confidently that I knew the document was on board. He went into a small room and came right out with a brown packet with my name printed large on its face, handing it to me. My glorious, wonderful, beautiful name!

In the morning the hotel clerk, who'd been born in Kos and knew everyone and everything, said my Greek-like fierceness had already made the rounds of cafes. When I walked over with my bag to board the ferry to Turkey, I was ready to take on the world.

*   *   *

Yes, small vessels as well as large can evoke memorable incidents. There was the reed boat that we volunteers at the East Bay Regional Parks constructed and then paddled across the Bay from Point Pinole to Angel Island. Replicating the experiment of Thor Heyerdahl in his Kon Tiki, our chief ranger named our project Kon Tule. The construction was of dried reeds from inland marshes. Some were split and braided into rope for packing and tying bunches of reeds around a wooden keel, the only non-reed element. This process took two months of Saturdays, and then we were ready.

After a ritual prayer to the four directions by a Native American holy man, we set off, seven of us, on our twenty-seven-foot-long reed vessel with single paddles designed for kayaks. We had to hold these oars up off the sides to avoid abrading the ropes. Second paddler of seven, I recognized that without practice in using the necessary muscles, I couldn't do this. And the challenge would be worse than expected: the rangers who were to accompany us arrived late, and so we faced stronger opposing currents.

Oldest of the seven, and a woman, I was too proud to admit what I knew was true. When, after fifteen agonizing minutes, a relief boat came near to ask if anyone wanted to be spelled, I simply couldn't say so. I stayed with each stroke, knowing I could not do one more, but then I did. Too weary to say a word, I declined again a quarter-hour later, hoping they weren't designing their approaches for the old woman.

"No, I can't," I said silently with each stroke. "But I have to. I'll ache horribly for days, but I have to do this." And somehow the nautical miles added up, and at last we were at our stop. We were all awestruck by the seaworthiness of our craft, and when we arrived at Angel Island, the rangers took children for rides—we were so high up, as if on a sofa, because the reeds were tight.

In the tent I took two Tylenols, and despite the clanging buoys slept soundly all night and woke without an ache.

A few days later, a New Jersey grammar school chum who was riding the (San Francisco) Bay Area Rapid Transit for the first time spotted a newspaper on a seat and was curious about the woman in the front-page photo who was holding up a huge needle next to what looked like a woven gondola. He recognized the name I resumed after my divorce, and got in touch with me a half-century after we'd last met. He had become a pharmacist and sculptor, and I had become a reed-boat paddler.

*   *   *

A small vessel I spent considerably more time in was Piero Spinazzi's gondola. When I lived with the Zennaro family near Ca Foscari University, Piero was my primary suitor, well, primary after Mario Ianicello, the enchanting dogano—customs official—who had three older sisters to marry off before he could be serious about a woman. Piero's sister was an actress and they lived in a palace on a canal. Each evening after post-dinner espresso at the corner cafe with gossip and political argument, Piero would bring his lantern under his arm. Law required that anyone going out on a gondola at night be equipped with a lantern. So all the habitués of the cafe knew very well what the rest of the evening held for this American butterfly.

Eventually I saw I was being used. Piero would guide the gondola with the long pole until we arrived out at the Lido. Then he would undress to his bathing trunks, dive over the side, swim for half an hour, then return to the gondola, dry off, ask how I was, and practice some English conversation before taking me home.

One night, after we pushed off, he wanted to stop at his house to get a longer pole (this was before I developed a sense of double entendre). He pulled up to the wall and told me to hold onto the embedded iron ring to keep the boat from drifting off. He'd be back in a moment, he said. Meanwhile, white purse on my arm to match my white pumps, I stood dutifully in the gondola. Almost instantly, a motorboat passed, pushing the gondola closer to the wall, but leaving a wake that pulled it away. So very soon I found I had to choose between holding onto the ring and letting go and drifting away. My position was swiftly changing from vertical to horizontal as I tried to link gondola and wall. But by the image of my grandmother seeing me this way made me burst into laughter that weakened my arm muscles, and I dropped—kerplunk—into the slime of rotting lettuce and condoms floating in the shallow waterway, white handbag still on my arm.

Piero was enraged when he saw that I'd let the boat go. He had to get an even longer pole to catch it and drag it back, then in disgust he brought a blanket for me. When Signora Zennaro saw the muck and vegetation on my dress, she screamed and pulled me into the bathroom as if I were seven instead of twenty-one.

The next day gossip was rife, with speculation on what could have happened. When I told a fellow boarder not only about Piero's gracious rescue but also about our Lido excursions, she spread the word. with so many embellishments and accusations that Piero stopped coming to that café entirely and had to find English conversation elsewhere.

*   *   *

Ca Foscari University in Venice had—and may still have—a long tradition of continuing the existence of a Doge and Doganessa (Duke and Duchess of the Republic) from among the students. One afternoon our Doge, a chubby and genial fellow with wiry hair and a keen sense of humor, ran over breathless to where I was sitting at a café and said that I had to go with him that evening. A British ship full of officers was making a formal courtesy call at the harbor and had requested two typical Venetian students to be their guests. He thought it would make a great tale to circulate among the students if he could pass me off as local. I decided in two seconds to go along with it, and met him near the ship for a few preliminary instructions.

The young British officers were models of courtesy, and the Doge and I ate more elegant non-pasta food than we'd dreamed of. We were surrounded by attention, and one fellow in particular was asking me to ride in a gondola with him. With my affected Italian accent I told him I couldn't go out without a chaperone, and so the Doge (who'd been born there) and two friends of his and I had our first ride in a private gondola, not the kind on which you stand along with twenty others for a few lire, but a tourist kind, with velvet tassels and an operatic gondolier.

The gondolier picked up what was going on. The couple in the back kept poking fun in Italian of the shy, stiff Englishman, and the Doge translated for the gondolier in Venetian dialect, which was beyond me. So I could understand the Italian but not the Venetian, and my date could understand only the English—mine with its fake "come se dice" (how do you say it?). Finally, the Englishman felt comfortable enough to put his arm behind me, to the amusement of the others, then removed it when it began to fall asleep on him. I conveyed his words to the Doge and his friends behind him. All this time the poor victim kept announcing what a fine time he was having. Not as great as ours, we were certain. When we got back to the ship, he said he never would have believed he'd spent an evening with a typical Italian girl. I didn't feel guilty at all.

By Air

In THE DAYS of propeller-driven planes, when jets were a Flash-Gordon dream, passengers actually used air-sick bags. My first plane trip was only an hour long, Bristol to Paris, but in that shuddering little craft, engines roaring like dinosaurs, half the passengers had used the bags by the time we arrived. Air-sickness has a way of being contagious, but I held out till we landed. Solid ground was not the only blessing. This was the moment when my push to independence from a small New Jersey town would extend to the Continent.

Breathing in the magnitude of this coup, I stepped onto the wooden platform with its steps leading down to the tarmac. I would not stumble, I would not forget my posture, I would always be kind and gracious, I would bring credit to my country, I would commit mental notes to memory. It was somehow, then, not a surprise to hear an accented male voice ask, "Pardon, Mademoiselle, may I take your photo for our magazine?" Gathering up my poise, I turned slowly to face him. Just in time, I caught sight of the knockout blonde woman his question had been directed at. Learning to laugh at myself was good basic training.

*   *   *

He was a combination of Gamal Abdel Nasser and the Cheshire cat. He was the Alexandria manager of Olympic Airlines, and as soon as we got off the bus, the other passengers and I, he targeted me. Have a coffee, where are you staying, do you have friends here, the usual. Then he offered me his apartment in Alex, which he keeps but doesn't use. Oh, boy, I thought, steer clear of this one. I was staying at a youth hostel and quickly developed a circle of international, mostly Egyptian, friends. But this was shortly after the Suez Canal crisis, and people assumed as a blonde I had to be German—no English or Americans would visit now. But I did, on account of a promotion run by Olympic, round-trip from Athens for an absurdly low fare.

According to this Olympic manager, I needed to file a report on where I was staying when I went to Cairo. He said that another foreigner had recently been found with a suitcase of propaganda against their government and President Nasser. Well, I had no propaganda or political intent. But I'd booked at the Ambassador and wrote down the Edwards, or something like that. What difference would it make? He was the oily kind that would find occasion to visit.

I rode from Alex to Cairo across the desert in a car with two Egyptian engineers from the hostel, and had a splendid time. We laughed the whole time about being too embarrassed to get out and urinate in the sand that stretched in all directions. In Cairo for little money I clambered up—and claustrophobically down—the narrow air-channel inside a pyramid, and galloped on a white horse around the Sphynx, disdaining camels. On arrival back at Alex, all the friends at the hostel rushed around me to say that "they" had been looking for me and asking questions. My friends warned that I'd better go nicely to the office.

When I did, the manager chastised me for misleading the authorities. After a few moments of sternness, he turned on the charm and invited me out. I declined. Then he said that although I had confirmed passage in two days back to Athens connecting there to Madrid, where friends were waiting for me, he couldn't guarantee I'd be able to get on the plane. I argued, if I have a confirmed seat, I have a confirmed seat. No, he couldn't assure a place—unless, that is, I went out with him. This was too flagrant. I told him I'd go to the Chief of Police. He said the Chief was his brother. I spoke of the U. S. Consul. He's out of town, a very good friend. I finally consented to go to the race track the next afternoon and sit with him for a while.

The next afternoon I showed up at the Alexandria Race Track and was warmly welcomed by the manager and his brother, the Chief of Police, in their box, with servants fanning them with huge palm leaves. The brother clapped his hands and coffee appeared within seconds. The two, who might have been twins, invited me to choose the winner of the next race. On the basis of an Afghani friend's name, I selected Fedai. And, what do you know? Fedai came in first, and my prize was a tour of the paddocks to see the most elegant horses in the world, their tails arched and braided like the tassel on a Greek helmet.

"Well, I have to go now," an old line normally accepted, but this time met with all sorts of questions. I had to attend a farewell party for me, I said, and they finally let it go at that. So I was free to wander around. It happened that it was the anniversary of President Nasser's overthrow of King Farouk, and there was raucous celebrating in the streets. I still have the plastic pin, commemorating the event, that someone stuck on my shoulder. What were the chances of my running smack into the manager? Well, I did, and he made no secret of his annoyance that I'd chosen to roam the streets over enjoying the privilege of his company.

The next morning, the day of the 1:30 flight, I went to the airline office. The manager came out to greet me and announce that the plane was overloaded with freight and I couldn't board. I argued, to his weird pleasure, until he said I should return in an hour. I did, and he had me stand on a scale and weigh myself, also declare the approximate weight of my small suitcase. Then he suggested I go to the beach for an hour and relax, and he'd see what he could do. The bus would leave for the airport from the office at 12:00. So I went to the hostel, where I garnered supporting moral outrage against exploitive authority, tipped the attendants, and hurried off with the little suitcase to the office, where I arrived at 11:50. "Oh, no," a receptionist said, "the bus always leaves at 11:45. You missed it." As she finished her sentence, the manager emerged from behind his partition and said, "But how lucky you are to ride with the manager himself in his Volkswagen to the airport."

The entire drive he delivered a tirade against Israel,

which would be "driven into the sea." I kept telling myself just to be patient and it would soon be over. But there was another worry.

During my stay I'd looked up a Greek couple, cousins of friends of mine in Athens. The couple had been trying to return to Greece, but laws prevented them from taking any property. They had the Phillips Electronics store on Khan Khalili, the main business street, and a home furnished finely—they showed me—and they would have to arrive in Athens penniless and dependent on relatives. They took every opportunity to get money over to Greece.

I agreed to smuggle twenty pounds for them, which had gone into a bra and a Tampax box. Very original, probably first place they look, but I was a novice.

Back to the manager, he took pleasure in showing the Olympic agents and officials a proprietary air. Evidently, I'd been "his" during my visit. My eyes were stinging with anger until I saw that the security woman ahead was poking into every corner of a woman's belongings, and I knew I was in for trouble.

As we approached the guard and female inspector—my heart hammering—the manager, my patron, patted me on the head and nodded to her, saying, "She's all right, she's with me, you can let her pass." So I did.

But before he turned back, I blurted out, "I've traveled to many places and met many people, and no one has made me more eager to go home than you." Being a pro, he smiled for the show of the crowd, and that was that.

The cousins of the couple trying to emigrate from Egypt met me at the Athens Airport during my short transfer to Madrid—another reason for not missing the plane. Like most of my Greek friends they had no telephone. The effusive hugs of thanks were sweet, but I never smuggled again. Not good for the heart.

*   *   *

Things might have been far worse. While at the hostel in Alex, I made friends with many young Egyptians, mostly students with a large circle of male friends, some in the military. We all went to the beach close by, with its very gradual slope out to the gentle surf. It was called Siddi Bysshe, which I thought was City Beach. One late afternoon, when we were still laughing and joking on our wide blankets, one of the fellows said he had to report to his military job at the wharf, and someone had the idea that I should wrap myself in a black towel and go in the car with him. They all leaped at the idea, and I went along with it.

The sailor said a relative of his was at the sentry post and would let us in without trouble. And that's what happened, as the sun started to go down. All one could see of me was a pair of blue eyes. Once past the guard, I saw hundreds of ammunition crates marked from Communist Czechoslovakia—not something intended, I suspected, for capitalist eyes. My companion left me in the car for a few minutes, and by the time we returned to the sentry post, his relative had been replaced. The new guard wanted to know who the woman was. I don't know what the answer was, but I do know that money changed hands, and we got back to our friends, who were merrily shaking out their towels at sunset.

*   *   *

Money changing hands in Egypt was a source of great interest to me. For example, I was in a car with a male friend when we struck a vegetable cart being hauled by a wizened old man. The poor fellow lay sprawled on the street but surveyed the vegetables strewn everywhere and scrambled to scoop them back into the cart. I was moved by the situation as I sat in the car watching my companion go out to talk to the injured old man. What I saw was money changing hands but no papers. When he got back in and started the car, I asked if he'd given his license number to the man. "Oh, silly American, of course not. He doesn't make his living selling old vegetables—did you see how old they were? He makes it by getting run down and paid by the driver. It's a good living, and he can use the same vegetables for many days."

*　　*　　*

I fell in love in India.

His name was Akhalesh, easy to remember because of its similarity to Achilles. He was eight, and he adopted me.

Our group of ten was fogged in for two days at Khajuraho, in the north, a very small town famous only for its erotic carvings on a late-discovered temple. There was nothing to do but stroll around and visit the temple, complicated and multi-faceted enough for a long visit or two. The paths along the street were of hard-packed earth, and animals ambled along as well as people. As I followed the signs to the old temple, I watched a woman pull back her sari in the most graceful fashion and not only urinate but defecate on the path, somehow never losing her poise or becoming self-conscious despite my nearness, avoiding the yellow trickle.

This was more exotic to me than the ancient carvings. Imagine being able to do that so casually.

I traveled on, and a youngster appeared alongside me and asked if I'd like his help. He was quite adorable and spoke enough English for us to converse. We talked about school for a while, and then he asked if I'd like to see his house. I happen to pride myself on getting into houses where tourists never go, in Turkey, in Greece, even in England. Being altogether certain that Akhalesh was a con-artist who made a habit, if not a living, picking up Americans, I found myself completely charmed by him, and by the prospect of seeing the inside of a local home.

We walked to a mini-village, with mostly women in the community square, hanging clothes. My escort led me to one door and invited me in with pride. There was a very old man squatting on his haunches inside the entrance—evidently blind, and clearly loved by Akhalesh, who introduced us. The man smiled into space, as we moved into the central quarters. Everything was of grey plaster. The room had been cleared of sleeping cushions stacked against the walls and was vacant except for the old man. The boy's eyes swept around, as if to guide mine, and then he seemed to swell with dignity as he turned, his arm sweeping the air, and announced, "And this, this is—the kitchen."

I looked where he pointed. It was the size of the normal stall shower, all grey masonry, empty except for a brazier on legs, a collection of ashes piled in the middle. "Ahhhh, yes!" I exclaimed, "the kitchen!"

I thanked Akhalesh and, with a lot on my mind about cultural differences, walked back to the hotel rather than the temple.

The next morning the front desk telephoned my room, and since my companions had all gone on what I knew to be a futile tiger hunt, I couldn't imagine who could be calling for me. "It's a small boy," the clerk said. I went down to meet my new friend, who was there with his cousin, a bit older, and we went out for a walk.

These wiry, bright-eyed children asked me for nothing but reveled in our day as much as I did. After our scheduled flight the next day out of Khajuraho was postponed, I wandered back to the neighborhood and found myself calling out, "Akhalesh! Akhalesh!" Everyone in the streets and doorways seemed to want to help me find him, and a girl finally did. He came running from wherever he'd been, took my hand and showed me other neighborhoods nearby. At the end of the day I gave him an envelope with my address and stamps and told him I would send him to college. His cousin explained what that meant, but I felt doubtful he would write, and he didn't. The tiger-hunters returned complaining about their rough van-ride, horrible quarters, and no sign of a tiger. "And what did you do here, all alone?" they asked, almost in a chorus.

"Oh, just wandered around," I said, wanting to keep Akhalesh a private sweet memory.

*　　*　　*

Another encounter with children was less pleasant. In Bari, Italy, where our ship stopped for a few hours, I strolled over to the cathedral square and mounted the steps. From the top I enjoyed watching youngsters in tattered clothing playing games up and down the stairs. I decided I would go to a confectioner's and buy a bag of cookies to give them. When I returned to the top step and held out the bag with a few in my hand to show the contents, four or five girls rushed at me, knocked me down, grabbed the bag, and ran away shrieking in hilarity. I don't know why I felt ashamed, maybe because, as a gypsy beggar beneath a Venice bridge once told me, paupers despise philanthropists.

*   *   *

Friendship is the greatest of gifts. Some say second after health, but I'm not so sure. Tristan Bunnetat is an email friend, a young chap in Scotland who keeps me informed on his girl friend, their noisy apartment, and their job-hunting, ordinary matters. We are unspeakably close, though we met only once.

We sat next to each other at Newark Airport's waiting lounge in the International terminal. It was September 14, 2001, and I had a ticket to London for September 12. For reasons burnt into history, the flight was delayed.

Meanwhile, my dear cousin Jay and I had watched the billowing smoke from across the river in New Jersey and lingered at the flowers, the teddy bears, the poems, the drawings, the candles—spontaneous shrines mounted along the park wall. Each day United's instructions were to keep checking, and finally on the 14th a departure was permitted.

I can't revisit this day's mood at the airport without a lump in my throat. The somber young security guards, the shocked pale faces, the uncertainty, and most of all, the wrongness of empty skies outside. Tristan and I sat watching the emptiness from the grand observation windows. Would we be allowed to take off? Would there be more attacks? What lay ahead?

At last a plane landed, and suddenly, from the United employees gathered at the gate, there came huge applause and hurrahs. They were greeting the crew and passengers who'd been diverted to Halifax, Nova Scotia, where they'd been cared for. A joyous, heart-piercing welcome, a break in the subdued gloom.

In another two hours our flight was announced and we paraded on. I am moved again, recalling in the face of each flight attendant the professionalism conquering grief, and the acknowledgment of "there but for the grace of God." They'd lost friends and partners, had swiftly networked and already held grieving rituals together, were in shock, and still carried on their duties. Many of us, too many, wandered to the rear galley just to be with them, exchanging knowing looks, and glowering at those talkative passengers who felt compelled to fill up the silence in this sacred setting outside the toilets.

Each Christmas Tristan and I exchange messages of cheer and affection. We don't talk about that day. We're not likely to meet again, but no matter. We are friends.

*   *   *

She was easily a hundred. I saw her clutching each chair-back, pushing full weight on her cane to arrive at the next. I wondered why nobody was helping her. But I was some-body and I had to act. It was a break in a piano recital in the twelfth-century St. Julien le Pauvre, with its high arches, its spare beauty, and a verger whose invitation out to coffee I had declined.

From the left aisle when I saw the ancient woman working her way to the rear. When after a few minutes I felt her returning, gripping my chair, I rose and said, "Excusez-moi, Madame, voulez-vous mon bras? Je peux vous aider." She hesitated, then gave me her arm, and we labored up the rows to the very front, where a coat lay draped on a seat.

En route she mumbled a few words I didn't grasp, except as we got near the piano, "piano." The lights went out and I slipped back to my seat, where I could focus on nothing else during the second half. The pianist avoided Chopin's delicate pieces and pounded away at the most fortissimo—a bit too fast here and there, with remarkable power for a slim young woman. Yet my mind was on aged women with skin like layers of wet paper and limbs that betray.

She must once have been the object of sexual desire, I thought, nursed babies, survived wars, lost her man, her contemporaries, who knew what more. And here she was with the final great pleasure—as I knew it would be mine—the experiencing of music. She'd scraped together thirty dollars and come early for a choice seat. Before the encores I began to wonder if I should go up and collect her at the end. I'd watch if anyone else did. Would she think I was a thief? A nuisance? Would I get stuck with a madwoman at the sidewalk? So I decided to ask the friendly verger, "Do you think it's all right if I help that old woman down from the front?"

"Oh, no, Madame," he answered with confidence. "She's the sponsor of the program. She can take care of herself."

*   *   *

In 1985 an airline named People Express tried a program of staggeringly low rates for non-stop flights from Oakland, California, to Brussels. I think the fare was ninety-nine dollars. That winter I took two trips over. What stayed with me after one was having watched three consecutive movies, two of whose titles I still recall, for some unaccountable reason, "The Jagged Edge" and "American Flyer."

The Boston architect friend I was meeting in Brussels proposed an idea. There was a movie he wanted urgently to see that afternoon, "Fred and Ginger." So off we went to the theater, but the billing had changed to Kurasawa's "Ran." I'd wanted to see it, but lo and behold, the subtitles to the nearly-three-hour-long Japanese film were in Flemish and French. That was the only time I ever slept through a movie, my fourth of the day, but who's counting?

*   *   *

How did I find myself hunting for a curandera in Mexico? It wouldn't have occurred to me to travel with Claire to the supermarket, let alone to Mexico. For one thing, I'm fond of lurking, and this Claire was one of the world's noticeables.

She was in her sixties—it was hard to tell—and was some kind of decorator. Her penthouse was done up to replicate a jungle. Mostly she decorated herself. Her perfume assaulted from twenty feet, her titian Louis XIV cascades inspired disbelief, and her parrot-green caftans swirled with every rapture over a passing poodle or a nibble of cheese. Her relentless delight put acquaintances somewhere between lingering to ridicule and running away. She was the friend of a friend of mine.

To be fair, one wouldn't expect a person with glued-on eyelashes to be versed in the Tibetan Book of the Dead, but garish as she was, Claire trafficked in the non-material, and collected parapsychologists and shamans. At her parties, her collectees piled brie on pumpernickel and sipped burgundy while they watched films of Russian psychics or listened with solemn faces to Claire's latest dream.

Dreams, she knew, revealed the directional signs on the pathway of healing and self-integration. Oh, Lord. In her closet there were cartons of handwritten archives of the twenty-six years she'd been dreaming for her analyst.

We had little to talk about. I once got curious when I thought she was referring to a lover, but it turned out to be her animus. Another time I told her I dreamed my apartment was filled with smoke. She was impressed.

"Oh, my dear. You're experiencing the suffocation of an emerging negative maternal archetype." The next day I found my chimney damper had broken and smoke was staining the ceiling. For some reason I didn't tell her.

With the practical facts in evidence, why did I wind up on a trip to Taxco with this person? Number one, it was a sensational bargain package. Two, Claire would make all the arrangements with her travel agent—and, it wouldn't surprise me, her astrologist. Three, she would pry me away for a change of scene from working on my dissertation, a pursuit that somehow qualified me as a collectible. And four, I'd just broken up with a sexy sheriff, my first amour after my divorce. Five, I knew some Spanish.

So here we were in Taxco, a seductive town high up, winding and cobbled, a refuge between the poison fumes of Mexico City and the poolside follies of Acapulco. And right off, Claire said she wanted to see a curandera, a healer-woman. She more than wanted, she became a blasted pilgrim, asking people in the lobby and on the streets where she could find one.

It was, of course, like asking around Chicago where you could locate a hit-man, please. We learned from one leering driver that they were illicit. And worse, Claire, not knowing Spanish, had to limit her informants to the tourist-oriented, without the know-how on retail rates for felony. I was sure anyone who did know the whereabouts of a medicine-woman wasn't about to yield her up to old Claire.

Whatever the devil I was doing in this scene, I have to say that I have a talent for salvaging pleasure. I liked the placid Mexican faces, the tasty new dishes and words, and the small-scale community. Claire's quest here was, after all, a little adventure.

And she wouldn't give up. One taxi driver took us to a pharmacist who scratched and shook his head. Then, of all people, a policeman, the type who look perpetually as if they're contemplating ravishment, gave his promise. I mumbled to Claire that the prospect of a sting crossed my mind, but she had faith and cash. He looked me over with arrangements in his eyes and said he'd meet us at seven that evening at the plaza across from the main church, and introduce us to a healer.

That's how we found ourselves sitting at the plaza, the policeman having found better arrangements, at eight on a June evening, watching women watching children from benches, as the red sun moved down.

Claire was desolate. With a bit of cruel amusement I bet her that I could find her her curandera by just asking any one of the mothers on the benches. Her face looked weary and sour. She was not to be joked with.

Then she brightened. It struck her, she said, that I might be the heretofore-overlooked source that the Grand Design had reserved for tapping at the moment of despair.

"Would you? Would you please?"

I gave the women a quick once-over and on a hunch picked the oldest and roundest. I went over and said, "Por favor, Señora, puede ud. ayudarme a encontrar a una curandera para mi amiga alli?" She dealt with my accent a few seconds, looked over at Claire, and nodded. Then she murmured something to a companion and I signaled Claire to join us. Piece of cake.

The woman was leading us, she said, to the very best curandera, who, by the greatest of good fortunes (oh, sweet Jesus), happened to live only a short distance away.

We followed white walls along two blocks and then slipped into one of those indistinguishable Latin doorways. Inside, the yard was lively with children taking us in while they went on playing, turning their heads from all angles, like cows when you enter their field. A teen-aged girl gathering clothes from a line said the Doña Maria would be home from church services momentarily. Our guide, refusing the pesos Claire held out, left us with assurances of miracles. Then we waited in the near-dark, absorbing the stares and self-conscious chatter of the youngsters. It was all quite nice.

So it was a Doña, not Señora, we were meeting. And when she appeared, small, slim, grey-haired, with a classic chiseled face, she was flanked by respectful women. She carried herself as though she were tall. Hearing my request, she agreed to see us the next morning at ten.

At five in the morning, Claire was at the wide-open casement doing some kind of spiritual preparation. Getting ready included having clean lungs and no breakfast, though she wasn't sure about coffee. After our few days together I was over the shock of seeing the stitches of her face-lifts at her wispy temples when she raised off the auburn tresses, and her torso collapsed in lumps when disencased.

I was annoyed and sleepy. "You can go by yourself." I pointed out that their level of communicating would be sure to transcend mere words. Oh, no, she wanted me along for instructions to validate the rituals. All those occult books on her shelves. I didn't even know what she wanted cured, though I recalled she'd once had some kidney operation.

The walls inside Doña Maria's house were painted glossy magenta, their only decorations a crucifix and two religious calendars. A partition bolstered by a wooden chest divided the front room, with its plain table and chairs, from the rear, which was taken up with bedding laid in bundles on the floor. There was one low chair she motioned me to sit on.

The curandera looked less regal today, in a faded cotton print dress. She had me ask Claire what her ailment was, while she twisted the lid off an unlabeled jar of salve and rubbed some between her palms like a pastry-chef buttering up.

Claire understood she was to remove her blouse and unbuttoned it while she told me what to say.

"My friend is oppressed by evil spirits," I translated, with a mental picture of my colleagues overhearing. "She wants to be free of a dark spirit that oppresses her."

"Si, si, lo sé, lo comprendo," the Doña said. Claire lowered herself onto her stomach and closed her eyes. She had on those damned lashes. "She gets it," I told her.

She whispered, "I knew she would."

"Women often get this trouble," the Doña went on, rubbing the salve into Claire's doughy shoulders while she talked to me. "It is a black fluid that has to be driven away." Claire looked at me. "She'll get rid of your problems," I edited.

Doña Maria began a rhythmic stroking from shoulders to kidneys which led Claire to murmur in relief and gratitude. Before long the Doña began talking to me in rapid, comfortable Spanish about her family. I understood less than half, but kept nodding with facial expressions I hoped were suitable and not a smile if someone's baby had died. Her husband was in Mexico City, trying to earn a little money, and she had a hard time paying the bills. Here it was, the pitch.

She kept on working. Claire, limp and sighing, tried from time to time to muster energy to praise the magic hands. I translated as creatively as I could, aware that a good massage never hurt anyone.

The Doña told her to turn over, and Claire lay on her back. I could see she was weeping. The curandera kneaded the flesh around her abdomen, asking through me if the pain was finally going away, and of course it was, it was.

I couldn't recall the Spanish for kidneys but asked about Claire's health. The Doña didn't seem to hear. She was telling me she'd received the healing power from the curandera who tended her foot. She held out her leg, smiling proudly. I hadn't noticed before that her foot was thick and malformed. I smiled and nodded approval while my stomach, caught off guard, took a moment to get past the pitying.

She turned Claire over on her stomach and had me tell her to lie quietly on the blankets for a few minutes.

"Ahhh, yes," Claire said in a feeble tone, "to soak in the power. Please, dear friend, remember everything she says, and give me the details when I'm more alert."

Doña Maria led me, almost on tiptoe, into the front part of the house. Pulling out the large bottom drawer of the chest, she showed me pieces of the family embroidery, unwrapping each article from folded white paper. It was remarkable work, fine and even. I offered to buy some.

Uh-oh. She was taken aback more than offended. No, they were not for selling, but she wanted to give me a doily she herself had done, to remind me of our visit. It was a beauty! I couldn't imagine why she'd give it to me, but I slipped it into my bag with thanks. Then, glad at my surprise, she looked hard at me and said some words about my life that I wished to hell I could understand.

"It really and truly works," Claire said as we returned to her. She was sitting up and stroking her arms. Now she declared that what she wanted was instruction to keep the good powers prevailing.

Doña Maria said we needed to stop at the church for the priest's blessings. "We work together, the priest and I," she explained and I put into English. I wondered if he'd turn her in without the kickback. Claire was eager to comply. She would light candles. Her eyes were still moist.

She fastened her blouse and tied a long blue-green silk scarf around her neck. Then she took two tight bundles of notes from her purse and squeezed them into Doña Maria's hand.

At the sunny doorway, Claire reached her arms around the Doña and clung to her. The Doña turned and quickly held me and let me go. I fought against looking at her foot.

"You have changed my whole life," Claire had me trans-late before we stepped out to the street. "Me ha cambiado toda la vida." We all waved and beamed, and that was it.

Claire and I walked across the plaza without talking. When we reached the other side I reminded her that we had to stop at the church.

"Oh, no, I don't think I feel like going," she said. In her elation she felt like, she felt like, she knew just what she felt like—some ice cream. And there was an ice-cream parlor right there on the plaza, up on a balcony with pink tables.

"But you promised her," I protested, in a volume that surprised me. "It was part of the whole thing. You have to do all of it, don't you?"

Claire laughed and tugged my arm. "Come on, let's have some ice cream. I don't feel like any dark, dreary church."

I pulled away, choked with disgust. "You goddamned hypocrite," I managed to shout, as if that were news. And I bolted up the hill toward the hotel. Claire wailed after me in disbelief as I put a good distance between us, calling back, out of control now, "Phonyyyyy!"

When Claire was diagnosed a year after Taxco, I present-ed her with the doily and told her the Doña had asked me to hold onto it for her. Meanwhile, I heard myself shouting in my mind, you idiot, Claire, we should have gone to the church.

*   *   *

It's convenient to use the resources of a (small, always small) organized group, A guide will know whom to tip, for example, to get out of the Khatmandu airport for a plane about to leave for Delhi. At the same time, except in perilous areas, guides generally don't mind if you excuse yourself from such group activities as comparing prices of kashminas. Many U.S. travelers see the exotic world as an extensive shopping mall, and my own style is to hang around on my own.

In our van making its way down the crammed streets of Jaipur, my nose was pressed against the glass. The street and sidewalk traffic included, of course, cows, but also goats, monkeys, even camels and one elephant! A barber was carrying a folding chair and a pouch with his tools and unfolded the chair for a customer on the street. Meanwhile, my nine companions had their backs to the windows and were excited about L.A. restaurants they'd visited, and how Donna Karen tights lasted longer than others. I couldn't wait to escape, and had a few chances.

We flew over from Khatmandu to Pokhara at the foot of the Annapurna range. There is nothing like the view of that range as it changes hues through the day with the sun's movement. One day I wished the others a fine time and wandered alone around the town. It grew very warm, and I needed to remove my silk Eddie Bauer turtle-neck undershirt, but there was no place to change. Finally I spotted two women, apparently mother and daughter, and pantomimed what I wanted to accomplish. Without hesitation, the daughter ushered me into her home and to one of the rooms, closing the curtain. How I love getting into people's houses in faraway places.

When I came out in a minute, I handed the shirt to the woman with a curtsy and effusive thanks, and the two looked bewildered and much amused. They giggled into their hands. My pleasure was immense.

Back at Khatmandu, the others having taken a bus tour,

I got on a local bus to a town I'd read about, Bhaktapur, with its elaborately carved wooden architecture and a pre-adolescent reincarnated goddess who comes to her window each afternoon. It was getting late in the day for good photos, so I took my modest fixed-focus 35mm camera, just in case something was not to be missed. I saw her, but out of respect I left the camera dangling from my wrist. There must be something to the notion of luck, though. A dozen of those photos would hang in a university exhibit for two years.

*   *   *

What could have possessed me to poke around a dark and empty theater one afternoon in Paris? The night before, at a piano recital, mostly Brahms, I was taken with the forty-seat salon on the Ile St Louis, its tiny stage filled by a piano flanked by two giant candelabras. The candles were painstakingly lit by a white-haired gentleman just as the performance was to begin.

As I wandered down the narrow passageway on the Ile at Quai Bourbon, I heard convivial voices approaching behind me, and found myself joined by a group of young musicians led by their mentor, the great New York jazz pianist Barry Harris. When I tried to backtrack, Harris persuaded me to sit in on the master class. I might help with recalling lyrics of the '50s for the vocalists.

After the class, Harris invited me to his gig that night at the Franc Pinot Jazz Club, down at the corner, in the second basement of the building where I was staying.

Another tiny venue—and I sat on a cozy stool at the foot of the stage, while Harris joked to and about me. His two sets were sublime, but as he began a third, ruthless jet-lag made me desperate to sleep. By chance a couple behind me deftly slithered out, and I took courage to follow. Up on the sidewalk, at a solitary metal table, the woman, Carine, was waiting for Pierre to fetch the car. Pierre had noticed, she said, that I had a fine face. "Yes, from behind," I answered, "and in the dark."

We had a good laugh and as guffawing chums over time, at picnics, antique shops, museums and bistros, often came up with cues for that refrain.

*   *   *

The trek to Jericho from St. George's Monastery is about seven kilometers along a steep gorge. The guide for our small group seemed to be a former Israeli military officer, a colonel at least—a barrel-chested silver-haired man of complete authority and confidence. I disliked his arrogance, though he said nothing particularly rude. We hadn't known what the trek involved, and although I wore comfortable sandals, it soon became obvious that I was lagging behind at the end of the line and growing more and more terrified. The path was two feet wide, in some places narrower, and the gorge was hundreds of feet straight down. My depth-perception is impaired by the unsighted left eye, and my balance is no longer reliable. At a certain point I froze, my knees unwilling to go on. The guide passed back an inquiry through the line, to which I answered that I was too frightened to continue.

His response was to edge along outside the line, with inches separating him from a fatal fall, and cheer me on with the promise of walking along with me on the outer margin for the remaining distance. My feelings grew complicated the more sure I became. He was protecting me, strength sheltering weakness, and I was at the same time grateful and resentful. I wonder if he had any sense of the second part, as I thanked him, of course, at the end of the trail at—ahh!—Jericho.

*   *   *

After a visit to Budapest and Prague in late 1985, winding up with friends in Vienna with their newborn, now about to graduate from Stanford University, I flew out of Vienna's International Airport and had my first encounter with high security alert. Two days earlier, Abu Nidal terrorists had massacred four passengers and injured dozens around the El Al counter. Passengers were exhaustively searched and prodded in a chill atmosphere of military presence that we could not have realized would become worldwide routine a generation later.

*   *   *

After thirty-seven hours of travel, I arrived sleep-starved at the historic Norfolk Hotel in downtown Nairobi, The cozy large bed called out to me to collapse there, but I'd made plans with a Los Angeles Merrill-Lynch agent I'd met on the long Brussels layover, so I showered, changed and left to meet him to explore the city and its nearby wildlife park—zebras, giraffes!

When I returned that night, I was beyond sleep-starved and nothing could prevent my collapsing. Nothing, that is, except for three pages of mimeographed instructions slipped under my door.

The instructions were baffling. They told the lighting people to arrive at the set first, at seven in the morning, on the road toward Mombasa, and the make-up people to be there by eight. The property people were to collect some hides and a Victorian tea-tray and set of dishes, and were to be very careful, the writer repeated, to be very careful, to return these items in the condition in which they were received. There was a fleeting reference to that prodigious lion-slayer Teddy Roosevelt. Evidently the pages were meant for someone who'd been expected to stay in this room.

The film company making "The Young Indiana Jones Chronicles" never knew that they had been saved a costly delay by a slumberous stranger with enough respect for the art of film to dredge up her last ounce of wakefulness to call the hotel desk.

*   *   *

An artist's co-op in Budapest had a trio of irresistible ink and water-color illustrations for a book of collected Hans Christian Anderson tales. The price was low for originals, and I was keen to learn about the artist, a woman whose painter-husband was very famous. When I asked if there was something in print about her, the clerk opened a large book with a full page, in Hungarian, on her life and work. With friends at home who could translate, I asked if they had a copy machine.

The answer was a definite yes, and the book was whisked to the back room while my credit card was processed and the three framed works were lovingly wrapped and tied. After several minutes I sidled over to the doorway to see how the copy machine was doing. A cheerful young woman showed me that she had just finished typing up a copy of the page and was whiting out her errors. Almost all the paintings I live among, like these three gems, have stories behind them that give as much pleasure as the art itself.

*   *   *

A university in Tokyo paid me handsomely to give two lectures on successive days about American culture. The first was to freshmen and sophomores, the second to juniors and seniors. The reputation of Japanese students was that, more than their U.S. counterparts, they are serious and disciplined. When they learn English literature, though, they talk and write about it in Japanese and don't learn conversation, so even when they'd read the books I referred to, they couldn't talk about them. The shock hit while I stood at the podium before 306 teenagers, and I couldn't keep their attention. When they talked among themselves I stopped twice and conspicuously waited for silence, then I progressed to a few remarks on courtesy.

It didn't work, so I just tried to make the lecture more spontaneous and turned to use the chalkboard. During the question period, it was evident that they hadn't grasped enough to frame useful questions. One asked if I was enjoying Japan. Two polite Japanese professors of English came up afterwards to greet me, and in talking with them I discovered they could read the daunting prose of William Faulkner but not put together a sentence in English.

There was one small victory in this scene. All the students had to write on the back of their attendance cards the one point they would be sure to remember. I learned that all 306 had drawn the four doors I'd traced on the chalkboard. These were an impromptu illustration I'd made of U.S. segregation during my lifetime. After all, I was paid by the university and not the American diplomatic services. I drew the four signs on the restroom doors I'd seen as a graduate student in North Carolina at the Greyhound bus terminal: White Men, Colored Men, White Ladies, Colored Women. I repeated, "Ladies–Women," in hopes that they'd get it, and they did. Hundreds of pens went swiftly to the blue cards. Maybe three or four also got my effort at irony in observing the waste of the station's space and plumbing.

After this somewhat disheartening teaching encounter I dreaded the next session, for which I'd prepared a more sophisticated talk. It was too late to rewrite it. My unforgettably kind hosts, Mariko and Keishi Tanaka, professors at the university, were troubled and embarrassed. They assured me that the second day would fare better.

In the lecture hall with more than 400 attending, Keishi gave a lengthy introduction in Japanese. And he was right, this time they paid far better attention, though there were no questions afterward. Later at dinner I asked what his introductory remarks had been. At first he said he'd told them that three questions on their final exam would be drawn from the talk. But I knew there was more, and Americanly pressed him. Because we are good friends, he relented, and disclosed something about his culture that moved me. He had also told them, he said, of their duty, after the students the day before had disgraced Japan.

*   *   *

While in Japan I got in touch with a student of mine from the seventies, Nathan (Yuji) Suzuki, my first protegé to go on for a Ph.D.—it was at George Washington University, tops in linguistics. He was now the most renowned linguist in his country, at Keio, arguably Japan's best university, and over the phone he invited me out for dinner. During my afternoon stroll (there was a tree that blessed an extra year of life for each time one circled it, and I got to thirty-six) and while I was dressing, I tried to figure out whether I should bow, as was the way at the campus I'd visited, or shake hands in the more American fashion. Still laboring over this choice, I was summoned by the hotel desk. I entered the lobby to be swept up in a hearty hug and off we went.

*   *   *

Our group of trekkers stayed overnight at a horse-ranch outside the remote Turkish village of Kemer. I chose not to go along when the van took off for a nearby town and market. The desk clerk answered my question about options to explore the neighboring forest by pointing out an interesting-looking road past a virtual metropolis of white beehives under the trees.

I strolled along the hundreds of stacked hives and on down the road, watching carefully for the way back. The one-lane dirt road was like a fish-skeleton, a spine with diagonal tributaries angling out. But some of these branches were as wide as the main path, and when I began to feel hungry for lunch and thought I was back on track, it soon became clear that I was passing trees I hadn't seen before. When I backtracked, I found myself even more lost. The mid-day sun was no help, so I tried following distant sounds of animals, roosters and donkeys, to take me toward where people could direct me back. But there were only fields of river-rocks and acres of orange and pomegranate trees separated by beds of rocks like baseballs, very slow to walk on, and all surrounded by forest. Some of the fields were at higher or lower planes, and moving through them involved climbing rock walls.

I stole an orange to slake my thirst and tried various directions without getting my bearings. It seemed that there was not a human being within miles, but eventually I heard voices of two women behind a row of trees and moved towards what turned out to be backyards of houses. I called out in Turkish, "Please!" When I repeated the word, loud, the voices became still. I could not make the steep ascent to their yards but stayed down in the forest waiting for any response. "Lütfen!" I called out again, met with utter silence. So I trudged on as the hours passed and I lunched on a fallen split pomegranate. I felt like an ancient sailor disoriented when the stars were hidden. I used my standard cheering line when a situation seems overwhelming—you're not going to be here next Tuesday.

Suddenly there was the heartening sound of a car. I pushed through trees to its direction. There was an ancient aquaduct between me and what seemed to be a road, but at a level at least eight feet above me. I hoisted myself up by one of its support posts and managed to arrive up at the road. But that car had been a rarity, and still there were no people, so I had to guess which direction to take along the road. I chose the wrong one, and walked about eight miles to a crossroad where a few houses sat, and at the tidy white corner house a slim young woman was sweeping the porch. I tried my word again, knowing that my other Turkish word, "Thank you," would make even less sense.

"Please," I said with a smile and my palms up, and she smiled back and invited me into her house. Then she turned on the television in the rug-lined living room, fetched me a glass with a bottle of cool water, brought out a bowl of sunflower seeds, and sat on the large sofa with the bowl between us. So we watched soap operas for an hour. She showed me around the house, a kaleidoscope of small oriental rugs on every surface except in the kitchen, showed me the family photo album, and pointed me toward the way back.

The only way I could communicate where I was headed was to imitate a horse. We both laughed and shook hands, and I was on my way. Past the row of houses a small signpost for various destinations told me I had only four kilometers to walk. When I arrived a staff person came over and said they had kept my lunch warm. In the dining room, there were my cohorts, assembling for dinner, excited to tell me about the souvenirs they had bought at the market.

"And how did you spend the day?" one of them asked.

"I got lost in the forest and then watched some TV."

"But there isn't any TV on the ranch."

"I know."

"Don't tell us you got inside another home. How do you do it? Just knock on any door?"

"Something like that. Yes. Glad you had a good time. Ah, here comes the food."

*   *   *

It must have been around 1980 when Keiko from Japan and Mohammad from Iran were in my class on discursive writing. Though their English was good, they were lost in the matter of argumentation, and when I assigned the class to attend a City Council meeting and take notes on the strategies of making a case, they asked each other, "What did she say? What does she want?" Their commiseration led them to do homework together, fall in love, and eventually marry and live together in a rented room. Because Keiko and I had the same birthday, we were close enough for her to keep me up to date on their romance.

When they graduated, he in geography and she in English, their visas terminated, so that they had to try Japan or Iran as a home. In Japan he could not be employed, and in Iran his family was not in good favor politically and she could not bear the burkah, so they moved to Canada, where he found a job. After a few years of extremely cold weather, he managed to find a place in Sydney, where I visited them and their two exquisite children, Minako and Nima.

At dinner one evening the children pressed questions on how we met, and that is when I heard of how my rigorous course was responsible for their closeness. Then Mohammad recounted something I'd forgotten. An annoyingly loquacious member of the class had dominated discussions for a couple of sessions, until I asked him, "What's the point?" He told us how the class had later cheered among themselves. For the remainder of my visit and in long distance phone calls after, four-year-old Nima shouted repeatedly, "What's the point?!"

For me, the point is that teachers never know the reach of their influence.

*   *   *

Air travelers are accustomed to hearing countless times that warning over the speaker system that goes something like this: "Please use caution in opening the overhead compartments as their contents may have shifted during the flight." On a South Africa Airlines flight from Cape Town to Johannesburg there was a strikingly pretty blonde flight attendant, living Barbie doll, with huge blue empty eyes wide apart and her hair done in two perfect yellow pigtails. At a certain point in the not-long flight, while I was engrossed in my book in the aisle seat, she came over and opened the compartment door above me, releasing a square hard-sided suitcase—bang!—onto my head. I screamed. The object came from nowhere, and felt like a box of bricks. Doctors had cautioned after my eye surgery to avoid impact

The young woman was annoyed by my scream and the attention it drew from nearby passengers, in the instant before returning to their passivity. "You shouldn't have placed your bag that way," she scolded. I told her it wasn't my bag—an irrelevant fact, it seems now—but she never apologized, and for the remainder of the flight pointedly avoided me.

I asked another attendant to send over the purser, who wrote a report. Being too familiar with regret at not having spoken up, I said as I exited, "Aren't you going to say you're sorry?" She looked at first amazed and then sullen. "I did," she muttered. An unsatisfactory form letter came several months later from South Africa Air, which is not likely to see me again. Since that flight I've always put my arms above my head when someone, especially a flight attendant, opens an overhead compartment.

*   *   *

That was the time in the air when a hard object fell on my head. But on another flight I had reason to fear being smacked by one. It was a one-hour trip on a small plane from Aswan to Abu-Simbel, where engineers in 1963 had sawed up and relocated 13th-century B.C. rock carvings, a hundred feet tall, to rescue them from high waters when the Aswan Dam had been built—supposedly to save Egypt from economic hardship.

My confidence in security arrangements was shaken when, after a hasty x-ray screening, we arrived out on the sidewalk among passers-by before re-entering the tiny terminal and boarding the plane. This casualness continued when about ten of us, with me the only woman, boarded and found no flight attendant or announcement from the cockpit. We were privileged to take care of ourselves.

All this was amusing to a degree, until I saw across the aisle to my left not a passenger but a roughly nailed together wood crate more than two feet square, sitting on the armrests. It wasn't strapped down or strapped in. It was just perched there, poised for a trajectory of its own. I wanted to hear that in case of turbulence, etcetera., but no airline personnel ever appeared—even the exit door was apparently controlled from outside—and the other passengers were not the fussy type.

So, weighing on the one hand a scream of "Let me out of here," and on the other hand, thirteenth century B.C., I told myself good things about a crate: it doesn't snore, it doesn't talk too much, it doesn't get up and bump past you, and it doesn't use an airsick bag. I counted my blessings, closed my eyes, and anticipated. My luck held out.

*   *   *

Assigned seating recalls a flight from San Francisco to Tampa, where I was to meet mon amour Bill for a holiday in St. Martin in the Caribbean. The flight was seasonably full except for the seat right next to me—oh, joy, I wanted to arrive looking rested. I would also arrive without a story to provoke his affectionate ribbing, "What happened this time?"

As the doors were about to close, someone carried a dangling-limbed young man to the seat and placed him there like an object—and his head immediately fell over onto my right breast. He had cerebral palsy, like my college best friend, and was living at Berkeley's Center for Independent Living—going to visit his parents in Florida. The depositor of this brave person had also left a duffle-bag at his feet, where the attendants allowed it to remain.

During an amiable conversation, he told me to wedge his elbow behind the armrest to keep him upright. Though I did this repeatedly, his head kept hitting my breast. While I learned about his program to become independent, from time to time he asked for little favors, like for me to reach into his odorous leather jacket and fetch some pills.

While other passengers dozed, window shades down, my seat-neighbor wanted ours open for the sunshine. And when the meal arrived, there was no alternative but for me to cut up the meat and feed him. He asked for a straw for his Coke, and when I buzzed for the attendant, she looked annoyed. I began to think, "Hey, I"m doing your job!" Meanwhile, I was suffering over flunking the test that had come at last, of whether I was truly compassionate or a hypocrite.

Well into the flight, when I ached for some rest, my companion, who suggested we get together sometime after the holidays (I'd passed the test!), asked if I'd reach into his duffel bag and get his urinal. That did it. I rang for the attendant and said the gentleman wished to be taken to the toilet.

The attendant glared for a moment, then suddenly seemed to realize something. She summoned the flight engineer, who without a blink carried the gentleman away. The attendant asked, "He's not with you? You're not with him?"

"No," I replied, "and please, is there a seat I could move to for a bit of sleep?" There wasn't, she shrugged in commiseration and apology. So when my neighbor returned, I feigned sleep, hard to do with the sun shining in and a head falling chest-ward.

The ending of this tale will be no surprise. In the Tampa airport lounge I flung myself into Bill's arms, as much in relief as delight, and mid-embrace he said, "What happened this time?"

*   *   *

Airline gods have otherwise granted me marvelous luck in seat-partners—handsome young men. And our conversations were often so pleasant that we wrote or saw each other afterwards. A gay M.D. from London came to visit in San Francisco and we lunched together at a Café de la Presse sidewalk table, then browsed down the street at the French Consulate's annual flea market. A handsome African-American football player talked of his aspirations and love for jazz, and accompanied me the next week to a jazz fund-raiser in my town, raising eyebrows as well as funds. There was a young Spanish banker, a Californian who had just toured French wineries, even an eleven-year-old traveling with his family from Papua New Guinea, who asked for—and received shortly in the mail—information on

Thomas Jefferson's Monticello.

The one I remember perhaps most vividly was Director of Exploration for Chevron, who was returning from Zaire, presently the Republic of Congo. In the long flight from Paris to San Francisco in business class, we dined together, napped together, drank together, exchanged tales of travel and family, and bonded happily—the kind of bonding that has no future but rests sweetly on the present. His photos of his family were a source of joy for him to share. Near the trip's end he rose and opened the overhead compartment, removed a satchel, and searched in it till he found a carved ebony lion—a gift for me. The lion sits on my dresser as a reminder that old gals still have something going for them.

*   *   *

In Luxor I had a medical emergency, an ink-like swirling in my right (sighted) eye, after smacking a hotel porter who put his hand between my buttocks. I needed, according to my California doctor on the phone, to get over to Tel Aviv for treatment. Cairo surgeons were good, he said, but the hygiene was problematic. He said that though the crisis was not a matter of hours but of days, I'd better get there soon. So I flew from Luxor to Cairo and stopped at the Hilton for the night, unable to eat or sleep and trembling violently. I called Heskel Haddad, a surgeon I knew in Manhattan, who had treated Egypt's President Sadat. He was out of town. Where was he? At the Sheraton Cairo, a few blocks away, where I paged and surprised him. I asked, "What do I do now?" He arranged for his mother to pick me up at 11 PM from the last Cairo-Tel Aviv flight and instructed me on the hospital and doctor, the same one Dr. Barricks had mentioned.

When I contacted the agent in Cairo who'd impressed me earlier as kind and genial, his concern was extraordinary. He brought me food though I couldn't eat a bite. He bought my airline ticket. He assured me he'd take me to the airport—anyone who has experienced Cairo rush-hour traffic knows what that means—and at the airport refused at the sidewalk to take the ten pounds I offered him. "I just want you to be well," he insisted, sounding very like my grandmother.

Of course I was moved to hug him. Let me hear no sweeping condemnations of Arabs. The Arab doctor in Luxor who'd spent an hour with me, clearing the telephone room to reach Oakland, also refused payment, blessings on his soul.

Inside the airport, passing SAS, British Air, Swissair, Sabena, Lufthansa, United Arab Emirates, Alitalia, one finally reaches El-Al. After the normal pre-boarding procedures I was unceremoniously ushered to a separate room behind the counter, where two severe-looking officials sat. They repeated the conventional questions, and then one asked, "Who was that man you embraced on the sidewalk?"

My answer sounded silly even to me, but I was confidently guiltless. "He's my travel agent."

"And do you usually embrace a travel agent?"

"No, but this one was very kind and did me special favors." It was sounding worse.

Their stance was between suspicion and neutrality, while I was somewhere between "What a royal pain in the behind" and "Oh, you fantastic Israeli security, best in the world at keeping us safe, better than anyone else knows how."

Meanwhile, I mentally retraced the long path inside the

terminal. "How did you see me?" I asked, and of course got no answer.

Questions followed on the nature of our relationship and they saw they were getting nowhere, that I had—oh, these Americans—just hugged a helpful travel agent. They returned to whether he'd been alone with my suitcase at any point or asked me to carry a gift. What gifts? When they ultimately seemed to lose interest and let me board, I was counting my gifts, none of them material, like being met at the Tel Aviv airport at midnight by a New York surgeon's mother. At that moment I had no idea how lucky I was.

The next day, two things happened worth note. First, Dr. Treister, of the sausage-fingers and shirt-buttons about to pop, used laser to weld on my retina, and second, the press announced that as a result of riots and fires in Cairo protesting an increase in the draft, curfews had been imposed, including a halt to all air travel for forty-eight to seventy-two hours, beginning at midnight, an hour after my flight from Cairo had taken off.

*   *   *

To get right to the point, I fell into an aardvark pit in Nanyuki, Kenya. These creatures, weighing up to ninety pounds, are equipped with formidable claws to dig for termites to slurp up. Often, I later learned, hyena families will occupy a used aardvark pit, but this one was completely hidden by tall grasses and unoccupied until my body crashed into it.

It was on an expedition to help save the black rhino from extinction as a result of rivalry with elephants for vegetation.

Bhaktapur, Nepal

Ernestina in Aguas Calientes, Peru

Friendly strangers in Peru

Along the Amazon

"Go outside, children, and play."

Princess Joyce and welcoming committee, Masai Mara, Kenya

Tea-time in Jaipur, India

Amazon village market

Turkish hospitality

Worker at Taj Mahal

Rear door of Taj Mahal

Nelson Mandela's cell for 18 years, Robben Island off Cape Town

Hair-stylist does coiffures at this salon in Turkey

Departure point for Loire Valley tour photo taken from bus

Air-conditioned theater, Nanjing

Abu Simbel, 13th century B.C. temple raised for rescue from Aswan Dam

Turkish Antiquity

Second TV installed, Cottage Hospital, Nanyuki

Hospital garden, Nanyuki, Kenya

The Big Island, Hawaii

Santorini, Greece

Home shrine, Akhalesh's neighbor,
Khajuraho, India

Iguassu Falls, Argentina side

New perspective on a familiar sight

Mysterious towers, Palmuk, Turkey

Cappadocia, Turkey, site of early Christian underground hiding places

Cape Buffalo, Kenya: "Beauty is its own excuse for being," Emerson

Masai Mara, Kenya

Adolescent male lion with non-related cub, Masai Mara

Sandal-smitten snake, Peru reserve

Darko and MK, 1954, hitch-hikers to Stratford-on-Avon

Elegant dinner out in Athens with newlyweds

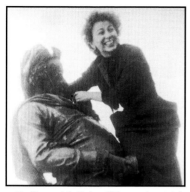

Fooling with Falstaff (statue), 1954

Transformed backstage in Shanghai

Countryside picnic, Greece

Exploring Aegean Coast antiquities, by land and sea

Alaska, reflecting on Al Gore

Aegean Coast

Laundry time in Akhalesh's coutryard, Khajaraho

Festivities at airport, Khatmandu, Nepal

Reed boat built by East Bay Park rangers and volunteers

Nanyuki is a four-hour drive out of Nairobi, and when I broke a bone in my foot, I was x-rayed and treated with cast and care at an unusual hospital called The Cottage Hospital. If there are such a things as living saints, I found them in the twenty-three rotating-shift nurses, who showered me with love and assurance that I would be fine. And I am.

Dr. Abid from Kashmir, pleased with his perfectly wrought cast, spent time each day describing his challenges—one day a demented parent of a colonial to be housed indefinitely, another day a leg gored by a wild buffalo. I suppose my injury was so minor, the prospects so favorable, and my spirits so high, that the staff enjoyed stopping by.

One day Fridah said she'd be off the next day and evening and would miss me. The next evening, she and her husband in the military came with a basket of ripe mangoes, to sit and visit. I loved these people, and they knew it.

A surprise visit came from the other nine in the expedition who'd carried on in their tedious work, with mediocre food and rugged quarters, with bird-droppings on the pillows. They brought little gifts, like a postcard from Sweden, and spent a while taking in the spacious room with English garden and gazebo outside.

They also noticed the two television sets. My second day there, after I'd mentioned television, two workmen went about hooking up a set, with wires outside the window to the roof. It took all day, and I could play their one video cassette, "That's Entertainment," but not receive stations. So they volunteered to take most of the next day to install another set, this one wired for reception. I wound up, in a country where people in towns might occasionally see TV in a store window, having two large television sets, one for video tapes and one for broadcasts.

All this while, Sasha Gainullin, the TravelGuard representative—a complete saint—was phoning me nightly because the hospital could receive but not make outside calls. He offered to call people for me, assured me everything was taken care of, kept updated with Dr. Abid, and made plans for my departure on British Air. Though I had crutches and the cast, I almost hated to leave this place. I'd come to know something of the nurses personally—two were recent widows, and schools for their children weren't free. During the nights I could hear nurses running a bath for an elderly woman with a baby's voice and prattle, repeating simple questions again and again, and I'm sure they didn't know I was listening. With the nurses paragons of kindness and patience, in an odd way, this was a paradise.

Sasha made detailed arrangements, and after abundant hugging, kissing and promising (I later mailed them two blood-pressure monitors), I was picked up and driven the four hours to Nairobi. At the last moment the business-like supervisor slipped into the van and propped a pillow under my cast.

Frankly, I never met a Kenyan I didn't like. The driver took me shopping for souvenirs in a roadside shop, haggling from the van window. He was stopped by officials at a jagged portable barrier—a shakedown, he explained later, that would have worked if I hadn't been there as witness. What they do, he said, is cite a driver for some minor infraction having to do with lights, and then hint that they'll let him off if he gives them something. It's a business, like the one of emptying and re-filling pot-holes while drivers wait.

At the airport he delivered me to the care of two porters

who carried me in a wheelchair up forty steps to the departure level. They were as attentive as the nurses had been, and, like the van driver, wrote their addresses on slips of paper for me to write to them.

British Air First Class is sensational. I enjoyed two of these flights, one to London, where I was wheeled into the First Class Lounge to use the computer, and the next to San Francisco. The press of a button makes a seat into a bed, with a pouf of down comforter and huge down pillow in old-fashioned white. I was the only passenger, and the two male flight-attendants couldn't do enough for me. I could order a meal from Maxim's at any time, and when I didn't want anything to drink, they tucked six little Glenfiddich bottles into my bag. They were disappointed that I wasn't hungry and wanted just a banana. And when the pain got bad, they helped me pry open the slit Dr. Abid had sawed down the front of my cast to lessen the swelling—not easy with only plastic knives aboard. What did we use? I think it was a pen. I slept more soundly than in any other air trip, as one might hope for the fortune paid by insurance.

On arrival at San Francisco I became for the first time one of those passengers who have their name printed large on a placard hoisted on a stick. It was a welcome sight, but also a curious one, because the limousine driver carrying it looked very familiar. He went to fetch the car, and I told him I was sure I'd met him. No, he'd been in a movie that I'd made much of and written about, "The Pledge," with Jack Nicholson, who had once asked me to his hotel room, but that's another story. All the way home the driver told me about the filming in Canada, the alternate ending, the problems of director Sean Penn, and other tidbits I relished.

When the driver had deposited me dutifully with crutches and luggage in my lobby, our smart-angel security guard Theo took one glance at the situation and whisked out a standby wheelchair to take me to my apartment. Neighbors cooked, friend Joe manuevered the chair to the multiplex across the street, and I didn't need to go to work, having just retired, or, as I prefer to say, declared victory and left. On the elevator, when people clucked with commiseration, I accepted it and kept to myself how glorious an experience it had been to break a foot-bone in an aardvark pit in Nanyuki.

*   *   *

Maybe it was because she read disappointment in my face, but the Principal Investigator (P.I.) for Earthwatch's Bali project disliked me. It was a women's group I volunteered for because my partner Richard was needed in Florida by his divorcing son for the holidays, and it was an appealing idea to learn how to construct offerings to the gods. As was my practice, I spent a few days in advance, first in Singapore, then at the elegant Bali Intercontinental, swimming, walking and running along the expanse of beach.

It came as a surprise, then, at Ubud, where our group met at the assigned guest-house, that when we were not confined to airless parlors weaving leaves, we were confined in a hot van to and from the guest house, with far too lengthy stops in town for film drop-off and pick-up and, of course, souvenir shopping.

The only means of exercise was to awake at six and take a long walk through the rice fields, greet the farmers, and stretch my legs before the heat set in. One morning I strolled as far as the Egret colony and happened upon a local artist, who sold me a splendid painting of Bali life in typical flat style on a black background. I enjoyed watching bands of children carrying brooms to their classrooms.

The only woman in the group I liked very much was, fortunately, my roommate Rell, an Australian who exuded contentment and confided that she and her Dutch husband had married three weeks after they met. Their grown daughters kept asking what their secret was, and she said she simply didn't know. Each evening she ran to the guest house office to receive her phone call, and returned looking blessed, as she was.

One of our assignments was to keep a notebook or diary of sorts to hand in for the P.I.'s review, and each evening my roommate would applaud my entries.

What I did not write in the notebook was that the P.I.'s resumé was false. It said she had been a professor at U.C.L.A., but without a Master's degree, that was impossible, maybe an adjunct lecturer. And she claimed to have published articles in certain years in a magazine called *China Reconstructs*. A friend of mine in China (what were the chances?) edited that magazine, and had written that it was discontinued before re-emerging under another title. Though I never uttered these doubts, they may have showed in my not sharing in the group's veneration of the P.I.

One day when most of the others went shopping, a few of us stayed in our rooms to read and relax. I was sitting outside my room writing when a custonian went in with his cleaning equipment and smiled on coming out, saying the room was ready. I stood—we were usually barefoot—and walked in. The tile floors in Asian countries are often highly glazed, as if covered with water. I remember that the lobby of the Shanghai Hilton looked as if it were coated with an inch of water. In this case, after a generous mopping, the floor was very wet. When I stepped down from one level to the other, I slid and went flying, landing on my back with enormous pain on the edge of the step. My scream reached the other rooms and people came running.

I lay in bed for several hours holding the card with the number to call in case of emergency, and when the P.I. came back, I gave it to her. I asked her to call and tell them the situation. Meanwhile, a nurse in the group plied me with ibuprofen.

In the morning the P.I. made her rounds audible as she checked in from one doorway to another, stopping at last at mine. I asked what the instructions had been: the reply was, "Oh, you completely slipped my mind."

I persuaded her to take me to a hospital for an x-ray, because the pain was intense, and instead of driving me to Denpasar, the capital, a half-hour away, she took me to a nearby village clinic, where the attendants were all in costume for one of the frequent religious festivals. When I was x-rayed, and the doctor said it showed nothing at all, I detected a slight smirk on the P.I.'s lips. I told her I had to fly home right away.

At the airport, with Rell along, I asked the P.I. to return my notebook. It had recorded ceremonies that struck us all as most novel, like the baby-naming ritual. I asked her to give them to Rell if she did not want to mail them to me. She promised she would, but I knew in my stomach that she would not.

After an excruciating flight, an overnight in Singapore and another flight, Richard picked me up in San Francisco and took me to my own doctor. When he saw the x-ray he laughed.

"This is entirely in the wrong place. They missed the broken rib."

The rib healed in time, along with the touch of pleurisy, but I've never healed from having my writing stolen. I wrote Earthwatch, who claimed to have no way to get it from her. This was not one of my better trips. But the first three days on my own were glorious, the painting is luminous, and I learned the skill of constructing offerings to the benign gods and the destructive gods, which always must be placated.

* * *

And then there was the plane that didn't take off. Our small group was scheduled to fly from Khajuraho to Veranasi, formerly Benaras, on the banks of the Ganges very near where the Buddha first preached. But the December weather brought too much fog, and our leader, Sanjay Chatterjee, couldn't get clearance for us to go. We waited for two extra days, with reports that driving along the highway was dangerous, and that bandits hid waiting to attack from the adjacent woods. At a certain point the travel company told Sanjay to go ahead by vehicle, and we split into two groups, a couple and I in a taxi, and the rest with Sanjay in a van.

Right away we knew we were in for trouble, when rain began and the non-English-speaking driver showed us he had no windshield wipers. He would stop from time to time, take a bucket, scoop water into it, and splash it onto the glass. Meanwhile, we were nervous about the woods and kept watching them.

Suddenly, pop, a blowout. He pulled over alongside the woods and explained that he had no spare tire. The husband of the couple went out to help him while we two huddled inside, with the doors locked. Somehow they managed to get the tire workable, but the husband was uneasy about the shouting from within the forest. It was surely a time for cell-phone connection, but Sanjay had explained that the government doesn't allow them on account of networking of insurrectionists. Baloney, I thought. He and the others were way ahead, having abandoned the two-car caravan security.

We eventually arrived at the holy city of Veranasi, where we slid and slithered around on cow-dung mud through narrow streets on our way to the Ganges. A beggar I'd just shunned humbled me when he saw me about to tumble and gently grabbed my elbow to steady me. Holy indeed. At the renowned river, people bathing and laundering along the bank, we saw body parts floating. Having just imagined ourselves about to be attacked, we felt relieved that the parts were not ours.

*   *   *

The other seven on safari arriving at Kenya's Masai Mara in a Cessna were eager to follow the migration of the wildebeests, perhaps their last chance of the season. But when I heard I could visit a chief's daughter in the nearby village, I opted to get acquainted with a true local and skip the wildebeests (gnus). That's how I met a princess named Joyce.

Joyce had gone to English school up to the sixth grade,

the level the teacher had finished, and communication was easy. News had reached her that she was going to have a visitor, and so my arrival was greeted by a line of women singing "Karibou," or Welcome, before they resumed their beadwork. We were in a small earthen area surrounded by huts, the central yard filled with children with noses dripping with hardened snot, goats romping, and the randomly accumulated feces of all.

I asked Joyce if she minded a tape recorder. She was delighted (I treasure the tape), and invited me to sit in her home for the interview. Ah, my personal triumph of getting into faraway homes.

I couldn't see but felt my way over to the bench in the wall, covered with hard dried animal skins. The only light came from a small opening in the ceiling where smoke wafted up from a pot dangling in the center of the area—with the familiar smell of onions, tomatoes, and beans. Was I in Mexico? Joyce explained that their diet for centuries had been milk and blood of their treasured cows, but a nutritionist had come by and taught them a better way. This mixture would be served with rice—yes, Mexico.

We moved on to other subjects. Did Joyce mind talking about men and women? Oh, she clapped her hands in glee, she would love to. Did she ever hear of the word "divorce"? "I'm divorced!" she answered merrily, then volunteered that divorce was very, very good. "A husband, he beats you, but a lover, he doesn't."

Then she explained her economy. First, you buy or get from your father four calves. You keep two and sell two after a little while. You get wealthy with the two you own, and trade one of them for two young ones. And so on. She knew she was on top of her game, and awfully pleased to be instructing me on economics.

When we strolled outside, the driver was there for me, and I asked Joyce if there was anything I could send her. She changed after a moment from efficient businesswoman to shy girl, dipped her head down and pointed to her wrist. "Maybe a watch, please?" Of course, the day after arriving home I sent her one, along with some etch-a-sketches for the children. I hope the watch arrived, though it was absolutely clear to me she was doing very well without one, this Princess Joyce.

*   *   *

In Corinth in the fifties, I was invited to help a bride dress. We used white curtains and applied her first makeup, black crayon on eyebrows. When I lent her my lipstick, I ventured to ask whether it mattered that she'd never been alone with the bridegroom. The question surprised her. Of course it didn't matter. He came from an honest family and earned a regular wage, and they'd have plenty of time alone over the years. I raised an American eyebrow, then raised two during the rites.

Someone snapped a photograph with a flash. The priest stopped abruptly and turned to the camera-wielder, shouting, "I told you a hundred times! This is a sacred ceremony! You must respect! You must not disrupt!" Then he resumed the sacred ceremony.

*   *   *

Christmas in Tel Aviv, 1985, as if it happened yesterday.

The day before, the hotel doorman watched me go out after unpacking for my first excursion and said, "It's getting chilly. You better go back and get a sweater." I got a sweater.

Where David Hamelech Street meets the sea I turned left and started walking briskly towards Jaffa to the south. The beach was empty except for an occasional white-haired gentleman—a Survivor?—sitting on a stone bench facing the mild waves.

Materializing, it seemed, from nowhere, a robust fellow in his thirties, sporting a purple and green Hawaiian shirt, began striding alongside me, beaming with affability, and introducing himself—he was Nate—without breaking our pace.

"I been to Chicago. Where you living?" he ventured. I ignored him for a good kilometer while he kept talking, but eventually made my blunder.

"You from L.A.?" he asked. Instead of reading a rebuff in my icy "no," he took heart in getting an answer at last. I was stuck. With an avuncular sweep he lifted the sunglasses from my face, polished them on his petunia shirt, and handed them back.

Then, how long was I in town, did I have a boy friend, the usual.

On one of the stone benches a very old man, wisps of hair disheveled by the breeze, was taking in the winter rays, his arms spread like wings. On an impulse I dashed over to him, calling out, "Mr. Birnbaum!" (This was the name of the travel agent at the King David Hotel.) "Mr. Birnbaum, how've you been?"

The old man quickened as if with recognition, "Just fine!

And how've *you* been?" As I neared him, we both turned to glance at Nate trudging back northward.

"I see you needed to escape from somebody," the old man said, his sea-blue eyes animated with a bit of mischief behind round metal-framed glasses.

"Yes, I want to thank you very much," I responded, turning to leave and not pick up another stranger in my clumsiness.

"You know," he said, satisfaction spreading like a blush across his lined face, "It just goes to show. A person can be useful."

I don't know if I made your day, Mr. B., but the rest of my walk to Jaffa was somehow all on air.

*   *   *

It's a great temptation to leave my seat on the plane and walk up to the small windows without seats blocking them, to look down on the glaciers. On a flight from London to San Francisco I went up to that section and found a couple embracing. "Hi," I said, and quickly turned away. I knew them, Gene and Eleanor, in their late forties. We had been in a group that summer enrolled in courses at London University. But Gene hadn't come with Eleanor, he'd come with Ginnie, who paid his way as well as her own and had to fly back early to return to work.

Eleanor, who wore cascades of curls like the Louis kings, had a husband at home and was on the prowl. Ginnie, Gene and I had bonded in London through our love for jazz, and when she had to go home, he stayed on for his first opportunity to see Paris. I went off to Italy and didn't see Gene until this moment, in the arms of Eleanor, with whom he had just spent two weeks in Paris, he told me. Ginnie was driving to pick him up at the airport.

Dealing with a dilemma is a high consumer of calories. Ginnie invited me to stay at her home when I took a course in her town—her three sons were all away at college. Her references to Gene showed she didn't know. So: to tell or not to tell.

I didn't. Here was my reasoning: it was between them. He knew that I knew, and I expected he'd clear the air with her. I didn't want my annoyance at him to drive my response. The dilemma reminded me of Sartre's reported answer when Camus asked which was moral, to join the Resistance against the Nazis or to stay with his mother in the south and find food for her to survive. The answer: "When it's that close, whichever choice you make is moral."

Some time later Ginnie had a phone call from Eleanor's husband. "Do you know that my wife and your boyfriend have been having an affair for months?"

They met to talk it over, and Gene was promptly out on his ear. The husband took Eleanor back—she'd done it before and probably would again. Afterwards, Ginnie suspected I'd known, and I admitted I had. It took a while, but she did forgive me. After all, there are offenses and there are offenses.

* * *

The extremes of summer would normally keep me from visiting China, but it was only June, and Eugene O'Neill scholars from around the world flew over to congregate in Nanjing and present papers celebrating his centenary.

O'Neill, it turns out, is one of China's favorite playwrights, and every evening we were scheduled to see performances of his plays in Chinese. The conference had been planned for two years, but what couldn't be planned was the weather. As luck would have it, the heat broke a thirty-year record for June by passing 100 degrees Fahrenheit two days straight.

We ventured from the air conditioned hotel only for brief people-watching spells and to buy folded-paper fans. The first evening we were to see the Jiangsu Art Theater's much-praised production of *Emperor Jones,* but our zeal wilted at the rumor that in China air conditioning was not turned on until June 15, just as heating was not turned on until exactly September 15, no matter what the weather. June 15 was a week away.

I spoke briefly with the Deputy Minister of Culture, a tough-looking woman who'd met me at the airport, rescued me from a sea of people, and escorted me by train from Shanghai to Nanjing. She stayed to supervise our comfort at the University, where we stayed in dormitories, awakened at five each morning by blaring taped music accompanying Tai-Chi practitioners in the courtyard. The deadpan Deputy Minister said nothing could be done to cool the theaters.

So the guests from Belgium, the U.K., Germany, Japan, and all over the States talked of how we dreaded sitting for four hours in a boiling-hot auditorium, with no translation, no intermissions, no beverages. Still, our hosts at the University had worked hard to prepare for the week-long events, and word got around that the *Emperor Jones* production was stunning. So we braved the few torrid blocks to the Xiju Theater, equipped with curiosity, dedication, and wildly flapping fans. We also memorized the route back for a possible early break-out.

I arrived at seven-thirty just as the lights were dimming. A ticket-taker at the door grabbed my wrist and tugged me down the aisle to the second row. What was that slipping and sliding? I held onto her arm, feeling my steps precarious on an oddly squishy floor.

When I got to my seat in the dark, my foot banged against an object. A very cold object. And although the theater itself was as hot as a room can be without spontaneously igniting, soon my shoes grew soaked to a refreshing—if not entirely comfortable—coldness. The bottom inches of my slacks, too, were soon wet and cool.

A tribute to O'Neill: slabs of ice the size of bathtubs had been placed at intervals all around the Xiju floor. The closer to the front the audience sat in the sloped theater, the more water they received from the melting chunks.

Here are some questions I can't answer: How hot would the room have been without this cooling device? How much did it cost to haul in and spread the massive slabs? And how high up would an official have to be to waive the June 15 date?

Here are two I can answer. Did I stay till the end? Yes, though in the second half I stood against the rear wall, baking like a gingerbread woman. And will I ever see a more brilliant and spectacular *Emperor Jones*? Not likely.

So, with easing relations between the countries, I hope to see the Jiangsu company bring its productions over here. I hope too that our hospitality is as generous as theirs, come hell or high water.

* * *

The temperature reached 117 in the shade that summer of '59. "Mad dogs and Englishmen" and young Americans taking advantage of a bargain flight from Athens to Alexandria could be found out in the mid-day sun. The Cairo hotel provided a shower with circular curtain and tile drain right next to the bed as well as the one in the bathroom, so one could stay half-asleep while pulling the chain for water. In the first twenty-four hours I took eleven showers The arrogant flies—right into your eyes and nostrils—and my first-ever bedbugs didn't help, and there was no place I could find relief. So in the afternoon I went out to hunt for any refuge and some mango juice.

On many street corners there were stands reminiscent of New York's Orange Julius or Nedick's. Friends in both Italy and Greece had warned me to avoid drinking any but bottled water in Egypt, so for the first few days I had drunk only mango juice and stayed well. This torrid afternoon, after I'd placed my order, instead of gazing off at exotic sights around me—the few people out were in everyday street garb of striped pyjamas—I let my eyes wander to the preparation of my drink. First the vendor pumped some concentrate into a glass, then he filled it with tap water. I didn't change my routine—luck seemed to be going my way.

But, for the heat, no apparent relief. The back of my blouse was sopping, and I could feel the heated air against my shins when I walked. Then, suddenly, I spotted a building that looked thicker and more solid than all the others, a squat box of a building with a plain flat ceiling. I decided to poke around inside, if I could.

At the entrance a uniformed guard was dozing, tilted back against the wall on the legs of his chair. A tight budget induced me to risk embarrassment, and worse, by tip-toeing past him into the rooms beyond. It was a museum, or more precisely a museum's storage place. I meandered to the back room, where my astonishment stopped me in my tracks. Spread out randomly was an array of gold items whose beauty took my breath away—in particular a mummy-case of radiant gold and faience blue stripes depicting a young man as if a mane of sun rays emanated from his head. A carnelian bird stood on his headdress, and his fake beard, as long as his face, was lavender laced with gold. His eyebrows and liner were blue and his wide-set oval eyes would hardly let me move on. Other items ranged to very small pieces, like a head-support and a gold comb, which another wanderer-in could have pocketed.

"People should see this!" I silently shouted. "It shouldn't be hidden in a stuffy storage room. No, the world has to see this!" I gently touched the Ginger Rogers figure, exquisitely gilt, of a goddess posing her arms outstretched as for a dance. Then back to the outer mummy-case, flanked by other less ornate layers of safeguarding for the deceased. I spent so much uninterrupted time lingering with these articles and gripped by awe that I forgot to notice until the end that it was about twenty degrees cooler in their company.

Two decades later when I visited the wildly touted King Tut exhibit at San Francisco's deYoung Museum, posters of my golden young man were all over the city. I saw selected pieces again, but from behind a velvet rope and glass reflections impeding intimacy. Yes, of course, it was good that the world was at last seeing the treasures, but my heart sang at the chance I'd had for a private viewing.

*　　*　　*

ing to Paris like a long-straying lover, I surren-
he fact that a once-adorable woman abroad in
her sixties had to learn new roles. France and I had both
changed since my twenties. Now the savoring would lack
the zest of inescapable male attention—the dentist, the actor,
the accountant, the government official, the interviewee, the
fellow train passenger. Adorableness had defined me. Now
divorced, no children, parted from professional context, I
craved to remain relevant.

True, my inner life thrived, nurtured by Bach, Socrates,
and the wondrous balm of sustained friendships, but my
social life was confusing. True, on my return, a youthful
charmer would materialize in step along the Seine, asking
rote questions and then for a phone number. And true,
within five minutes a creaky avuncular War veteran would
join me at the BHV Cafe. But the sparkle of real possibilities
had waned. Older men seemed either paired or impaired.
Flirting struck me as grotesque. Would I now be reclusive?
Scholarly? A tribal elder? Natural? What would natural look
like?

I'd play it case by case until a new mantle eased onto my
shoulders.

My first excursion was a bus tour of medieval castles and
chateaux in the Loire Valley—bearing romantic names like
Chenonceau and Chambord, with stops for refreshment and
a lunch at Amboise. The bus would gather passengers from
hotels at the sadistic morning hour of seven and return us at
nine in the evening, a marathon day.

No communication passed among the thirty of us the
first two hours, even those traveling together. Although I
never glanced at the fellow passengers, I gathered most were

Americans. At the first profoundly-welcome coffee stop, I found myself joined by a man about my age, a former New York lawyer now living his second life in Brazil. He looked a bit like a shorter DeNiro with a larger nose. His name was Harry.

Harry volunteered over cappuccino and crumbly almond croissant his rapture over a wife in her twenties and a two-year-old son, his frenetic Manhattan existence with ex-wife and law partner Sylvia but a memory. He asked if he could sit with me at lunch and I agreed—why not? Though I nursed some resentment toward men nesting with females younger than their daughters, I'd come to appreciate that the culprit was Mother Nature more than the fellows who exploited her.

I found myself attentively companioned. In strolls through the castles as we half-listened to the guide's robotic recital of dates, origins, and architectural facts, Harry and I exchanged Yogi Berra and Lady Day anecdotes. We'd both seen Coleman Hawkins at the smoky Metropole on Broadway. Alternating with these tales were his reports of how satisfying his new life was.

At lunch passengers from Ohio and South Carolina gave us a wide berth as we gorged, along with sole meuniere, on names and issues: Peter Lindsay, Sinatra, Kissinger, Roe v. Wade, Ed Sullivan, Ed Koch, SNCC, Jimmy Durante, Pol Pot, the Russian Tearoom, the Stork Club, rent control, Sonny Rollins, Yankee Stadium. At a few points he became wistful, then returned to praising Rio's vibrant ambience.

During further stops and rambles through portrait-lined corridors and sunny gardens, cracks in Harry's portrayal of delight with Rio wife and baby widened. They widened so alarmingly that, with nothing personal at stake, I became solicitous, as one does when watching any collapse.

On the stretch back to Paris in the darkened bus, the passengers dozing, my new chum slipped into a state of distress, struggling against tears. When the brakes squealed more frequently as we arrived at the city's outskirts, he sighed deeply. He looked past me out the window and said that the day had opened a wound, reminding him of all that he'd given up. His young wife (never named) understood nothing he had to say, he had no patience with the child or his wife's grasping family, he yearned for a civilized person to talk with, about anything, and he was in a trap of his own making. . . .

We didn't exchange last names or addresses. What would be the point? We shook hands before I descended at the Hotel de Seine.

My feelings were mixed. Harry had made the day-tour far more than an excursion of the Loire Valley. His suffering seemed genuine, and I was in no position to judge foolish romantic choices. Too, I'd glimpsed another handling of the challenge of passing sixty. And, as it came to me back in my room, his compliment had shed light on the wealth of new roles of an older woman. I looked in the mirror and saw—a woman of substance.

And one who was not only relevant but a downright menace.

*   *   *

At a sprawling animal ranch in Peru, something between a sanctuary and a zoo, with fenced sections for a variety of species, the most popular feature was a boa constrictor that was said to weigh 240 pounds. It was stretched out lolling in a loose S on the grass. One large Texan wanted a photo with it on his shoulders, and the guide and a park attendant obliged by lifting it onto his staggering body just long enough for his wife to get the shot.

I just wanted a photo. The problem was scale, the proportion of object to context. In Tahiti I had photographed a spider on the bathroom wall that was as large as a salad plate. But on the developed print, the spider could have been an inch or less in size, so I realized I needed some other item in the frame.

When the attendants had eased the unfazed serpent into its grassy area and beckoned me to go ahead and take my photo, I slipped off a white leather sandal and nudged it through the fence close enough to solve my scale problem. Click. And I can show now how huge the boa was.

But a new problem arose. The snake liked my sandal, and kept it, may be keeping it still, since it has no food value and the boa's diet is probably a pig or twenty chickens at a time. The boa simply snuggled, not too tightly, almost protectively, near the shoe.

The attendants had departed for a crisis with an injured ostrich, and my guide was hurrying me to our van, to which I hopped on one foot. It's a sweet thought, though. Somewhere in the world there is a creature who cherishes the scent and memory of my visit.

* * *

By Rail

MY EARLIEST MEMORY is of waking at night to the hoot of a train during a visit with my mother to her brother in Philadelphia. Many decades later, the sound of trains every night from the nearby Amtrak station brings the same balance of safety and adventure. The rumble-wheeze-hiss-and-toot proclaims that people are on the move from somewhere to somewhere. And the factor of uncertainty gives that movement an edge.

*　*　*

They were out of central casting—as longshoremen, bouncers, perhaps pirates. Heads shaved, cigarette packs tucked into sleeves of striped jerseys over formidable muscles. One was tall, the other stocky, and each bore a conspicuous gold tooth. Not the likeliest candidates for me to spend the night with.

The ship from Piraeus had landed in Brindisi for a train connection to Rome, and the station was crowded. I hadn't thought of the Easter holiday, as had the crowd on their pilgrimages to the Holy City, where I was going merely to visit a friend. It was 1955. I carried my Olivetti portable typewriter, a small off-white artificial leather suitcase bought at half-price, and a brown handbag with a strap that abruptly broke in front of everyone, leaving the bag dangling on end.

The two Greeks approached me and for some reason I trusted when one of them made clear he would fix it if I'd hand it over. That was first in a series of uncharacteristic risks with these two. The taller one quickly produced a heavy needle and thick thread and began to stitch. When the job was done they introduced themselves as merchant marines on holiday—one, I think, was a cook—and I thanked them earnestly. A bond somehow got forged. We had coffee at a small table, exchanging family photos and names. Without a language in common, people do invent ways to connect.

As passengers swarmed to the train, it became evident that it could not reasonably hold the number trying to board. It was also evident that I had acquired a pair of guardians. With my belongings in hand, they pushed past the many passengers already seated on their suitcases in the corridors from earlier stops in the south, their sandwich-leavings and orange peel scattered to step over. The duo checked quickly in each compartment, car after car, signaling to each other the dismal results. But my hunch was that some strategy was being cooked up.

When they slid shut the last door of the third-class carriages, they came upon plush compartments with random spaces and ultimately an entirely empty car, with red velour upper and lower bunks. They threw in their sacks and set down my things, nodding to indicate one whole side for me. Then they stood at the doorway glowering, arms folded, menaces to the crush of passengers now forced to resign themselves, in the absence of any conductor, to accepting the three of us occupying a compartment while all the rest were crammed with six or eight. I never saw a conductor during the trip. People had fallen asleep on their rope-tied belongings, leaning against the metal corridor walls. That was where I would be if not for my protectors.

Well, now what? This was an all-night journey. The shades to the corridor were lowered. I watched and waited, somehow less afraid than I should have been. I recall the scene clearly. My escorts became nurses, folding my coat into a pillow and showing me that they would occupy the other side and continue to keep out the rabble. When it grew dark outside and we had shared their bread, meatballs and fruit, we took turns to the WC at the end of the car. One guardian left to deal with new intruders outraged to discover our luxury when they slammed open the glass doors, until one by one they saw it was hopeless.

My companions fashioned a blanket of jackets, and spoke softly when they spoke at all. I slept. I slept well, in fetal position facing the strangers, my hands folded under my head and above my coat-wrapped purse. I slept so well that I never heard the men leave to shave and brush their teeth. When I sat up, apparently rested, their faces bore the mild smiles that grandmothers wear. I had been reading a novel by Andre Gide that pursued the idea of the gratuitous act, a kindness without prospect of reward. When we parted, with lively pantomime of fellowship, at the station in Rome to go on our different ways—would they ever have heard of Gide?—I was left with a tangle of impressions about appearances and the vast mysteries of kindness.

*   *   *

Metal screeched to a dead stillness in Trieste in a wide river of tracks, twelve across. We sat there without explanation. Or rather, I sat there, alone, and waited. Ten tracks across was the engine of another train, the engineer up high grinning and gesticulating from his window, pointing to himself and to me, then back to his heart, then palms together supporting his tilted head, as if in blissful repose. I looked away, turned my back, took out a book, in every way shutting out the clown until he seemed to give up.

I expected the train to start up again. What I didn't expect was a small boy rapping on the compartment glass fifteen minutes later, then entering with a spray of purple flowers, reaching them out to me ceremoniously, pointing over to the engineer, then running off. Holding the bouquet, I glanced over at the source, and there he was, hugely pleased with himself. I nodded approval toward the flowers, assured by the train's slow procession that I could now smile, as the train—and my unpredictable little life—began to resume its course.

*   *   *

Only a week earlier, trains and flowers had linked together in another episode. In Athens Spiros told me a sad tale of his cousin Nick in Salonika. Nick had been cruelly disappointed a few years back, discovering his fiancée was taking costly gifts from an admirer she was secretly spending time with. He was still suffering and trusted no one. When I'd left Athens laden with cold chicken and meatballs prepared by Spiros' wife Maria, I felt queasy about the invitation from Nick and his mother to stop there a few days on my long trip northward toward Frankfurt.

Yet the three days were pleasant enough. Nick was not physically attractive, a hyper-serious, roundish type, but I listened to him appreciatively. Yes, betrayal is hell. Meanwhile I saw all of the Salonika region and learned about its culture. I was treated kindly by the family, who gave the impression of scrutinizing me. Finally, I seemed to have won the trust of son and mother, not for any immediate purpose, but some larger idea, signified by their calling me "a good girl."

As I climbed up the train steps, Nick presented me with a box. I had just enough time to peek inside and find pure white lilies of the valley. I offered him an understanding glance. Yes, the purity that he wanted desperately to believe existed might exist. All the way to Zagreb, where I would visit a few days with an old school chum, Darko, I thought about Nick's story and his still-evident grief, and I looked forward to enjoying the flowers.

At Zagreb the train had hardly stopped when I saw Darko approaching on the platform with a blue and yellow bouquet. In no time at all he was before me in the compartment, greeting, embracing, talking, as he reached for my suitcase. He nodded towards the box on the shelf above and asked if that was mine as well. I yearned for at least another glance at the symbolic blossoms but couldn't bring myself to claim them. "No," I answered, wondering if I'd ever forget my dismissal of Nick. That was in 1959, and I haven't. But as I write this, I suddenly discover that of course some passenger in that seat had to be in for a fragrant surprise.

*   *   *

When my difficult cousin Paul was stationed at an Army base near Frankfurt, Germany, in the late fifties, he became romantically involved with a beautiful young woman who eventually had a baby after he left for home. When he heard I was passing through Europe by train en route home from Greece, he asked me to stop by the village where she lived, to see the baby and, more importantly, see if it resembled him, in which case he would authorize me to ask her to marry him. I picked up a cheap camera and two rolls of film, one to take home with me.

The route was slow and tedious—I needed to get off the train at Frankfurt and change for Fulde, then wait for a local train that would take me to Rommers. The family had no idea I was coming, or even of my existence, but I expected them to be at home. When I got off the train at Rommers, knowing just enough German to get by, there was one taxi, which was the town's only automobile among the ox-carts, and it was driven by the Mayor. As he opened the car door, he told me he knew where I was going and would take me there. At the gate of the house I asked him how he could possibly know. He said, "Easy. There is only one family in this town where any American has ever visited."

At the front door I was met by a jovial, leathery man of about fifty—I'd heard the father was a woodsman. When

I introduced myself as Paul's cousin, he pumped my hand affably and whisked my valise inside. Marta, he said, was at work in Fulde, but his wife was changing the baby in the other room, where he promptly led me.

The baby was a writhing little female replica of my cousin.

With much ado I was invited to stay for as many weeks as I wished. While I waited with them for Marta to get home, I asked about the bathroom and was directed to a door downstairs under the house. It turned out that there were two doors, and when I opened the first, a brown cow stuck its head out to greet me. The second was the outhouse, or underhouse. The mother explained that the family takes turns bathing at the kitchen sink, then took me to a cozy upstairs room with a dormer window open to the freshest air I have ever smelled, and an inviting feather bed.

Marta was the only family member who spoke English. After she joined us, soon followed by her brother, I took photos all around but mostly of baby Andrea, and we all had supper in a merry mood. The next day the weekend began, so Marta and I took Andrea out in her elegant pram. People in town greeted her without a trace of condescension for having fraternized with a U.S. soldier.

Finally the moment arrived to do something I'd never done before and don't expect to again—propose marriage. I volunteered with more hope than certainty that my well-off aunt and uncle would receive her warmly. We walked for perhaps a block further, exchanging nods and "Tag" with passers-by, before she stopped to answer.

"No," she said, and slowly tapped the side of her head three times. "No, because he thinks too much." She stood there, a farm girl not yet twenty with a job in a hat factory, displaying uncommon wisdom. She had pegged him, and she knew who she was.

*   *   *

Working my way up the east coast of Spain and unable to afford the more fashionable Ibiza or Mallorca, I thought I would spend a few days on the less expensive Costa Brava, where I found a modest motel right on the beach. After a long train journey, I was eager to get to the blue sea. I attached my room key to my wrist on an elastic band and left my towel and sunglasses near one of many small dunes that broke up the nearly empty stretch of sand. I saw no other towels or bathers around as I gauged where I was, in case the current swept me some distance from the motel.

It was a long, glorious swim in clear blue temperate water. I can't recall enjoying one more. And my guess was right—the current had drawn me southward, so that I had to trudge along on the hot sand to locate my blue towel. When I finally saw it from behind a dune, I froze in disbelief. A man with a huge belly and greasy black hair was on my towel, and he was vigorously masturbating with my sunglasses.

I went to the room, quickly showered, packed, retrieved my passport from a surprised desk clerk, and walked all the way to the train station for a four-hour wait till the next train north. I'd forfeited a night's hotel bill and an attractive pair of sunglasses, but I felt I'd lost something inexplicably more precious.

*   *   *

Much as I distrust generalizing, I maintain that Italians are animated with such gusto that they can make any small incident into an opera. I adore Italy.

I had spent the day visiting Verona, and as planned took the last train back to Venice, where I was living. Arrival time was midnight, and my friends, Italian and always worked up about my safety, would meet me there.

On the train the occupants of the compartment shared vigorous handshakes, energetic conversation, their sandwiches of salami and cheese, and exchanges of address. The nun opposite was especially genial. They were all interested in what an American was doing living in Venice, and we passed photographs around—in other words, the typical sojourn.

I was beginning to doze when I started at the train's noisy slowing—my watch showed nearly midnight, which must mean Venice. So I shook hands around in haste, and, as the train screamed to its stop, I stepped down and strode forward along the platform, concentrating on waking up and looking for my friends. It took only a few seconds to become aware of the absence of crowds and of the sign reading "Mestre," the last town before Venice. I had got out too soon. But that was the last train. Did I mention that at that time I was living on room and board for a dollar-fifty a day?

The train was starting to move when I slid my handbag strap up my arm and grabbed onto the handrails of a ladder leading up to the caboose and pulled myself up. Good, I was in the caboose and the engineer was scolding me but with amusement. His assistant escorted me, with much conversation about his unmarried son, back through a mountain of mail in the second car. As the train gained speed he tried to set up a meeting between his son and me. I told him I was betrothed. After warm handshakes, I made my way back to the original compartment and slid open the glass door.

Madonna mia! Incredibile! Non é possibile! She's like a ghost! How did she do it?! They all stood up, surrounding me with questions. I offered my easy explanation, but this would not satisfy their astonishment, and when we descended shortly after in Venice, they all followed me, the nun included, to my group of friends. Without waiting for an introduction, they regaled them with the amazing tale of the young woman who left a train—they saw her go with their very own eyes—and returned while it was speeding along. I adore Italy.

*   *   *

For four days in Munich I lived on two slices of brown bread and coffee in the mornings in an "ein bett zimmer." It was August, ten years after the War's end. London still had whole city blocks blasted out by Nazi bombs, with link chains marking off the craters. My Fulbright check had been misdirected, and the U.S. Consul told me they'd tired of indulging youthful American travelers with loans. Anticipating the check would reach the American Express office, I took advantage of Munich's policy of rotating free days among its museums. Looking at paintings and walking around the attractive city was an effort to keep my mind off food.

On the fourth day, not quite hallucinatory but a little susceptible, I strolled through a park and grew curious about some well-dressed Germans walking purposefully together. They paid no attention when I joined them as if I belonged.

Before long we reached a massive marble table-like slab

propped up by slabs on their edges with steps descending below it. There lay in bronze effigy Germany's Unknown Soldier, wearing that familiar despised helmet. The figure of the young man in repose moved the group palpably as my stare fixed on that abominable helmet,

Was it the hunger and disorientation that helped open my heart? Along with the others I found myself weeping as they spoke quietly among themselves about Gott. We were still at a point when respecting the enemy dead would incite such feelings of betrayal that I would never tell my family. Who was this Gott, and how did he let all of it happen?

*   *   *

Always short on cash, living on a graduate fellowship that paid $2,000 a year, I nevertheless scrimped to take the train from North Carolina to New York and stay at a cousin's just to see one performance. My friend Alan Rankin was a prolific author of magazine articles under various pseudonyms, including, for the *Reader's Digest,* "The Most Unforgettable Character I Ever Met." In 1956 he would give rollicking parties at his Chapel Hill home. At some point during a party he'd go into his study for an hour or two and come out with a large beige envelope to take to the Franklin Street Post Office, remarking on his way out the door that the article he'd just finished would bring in $2,000.

Alan told me he wasn't the most talented in his family. In fact, whenever I would next visit New York, I'd have to meet his sister, Nell, a mezzo-soprano at the Met. Not long after, I made "whenever" happen and packed my bag. Nell was playing Azucena in "Il Trovatore." Alan had arranged a backstage visit after the performance, so when the only available ticket was for standing-room high up, I was too shy to ask for a comp. It would be fine to shift weight from leg to leg among a contingent of music students in the second balcony.

Just as the orchestra members took their places, a dapper-looking gentleman, a dead ringer for Clifton Webb, came over, gently tapped my arm, and offered me a vacant seat next to him in the section's front row. The students around me watched with curiosity and perhaps envy when I followed the gentleman as the hall grew dark.

And how dark it was, and how quickly a hand migrated to my knee, a hand that I reflexively brushed away. It returned and I pushed it away. This annoyance persisted till it seemed spectators behind us must be observing the mini-spectacle. I would have returned in embarrassment to standing-room, but moving would have been disruptive—an alternate spectacle. For the whole first act, then, I was attentive at the same time to hearing glorious music and shoving away the intrusive hand.

The moment the applause began I sprang from my seat to rejoin the students, who were cheering too wildly to notice my slinking return. This was the fifties, and I felt shame, as I had when Mr. Keller, my boss at the Philadelphia Evening Bulletin, had grabbed my behind whenever he could. The only recourse was to quit—in shame. The rest of the performance was sublime, and all of us standees agreed that Nell Rankin as the gypsy was incandescent. We'd never heard singing like that.

As the audience milled towards the exits, and I reflected on the irony of the gypsy's switched sons, I suddenly felt an arm locked with mine—the boor had taken possession of my elbow, marching me in lockstep down the many stairs and announcing that we would be going to the Russian Tea Room.

I wasn't able to escape his grip when we reached the crush in the foyer, but outside at the corner I pulled to the left and around to the side of the building. He stuck close at my side in the thinning crowd over to the stage door steps, where a uniformed guard at the top was holding a sheet of paper. I leaned over and muttered my last name. Checking down his list, he nodded approval, then, following my scowl and head-gesture, blocked the Clifton Webb look-alike from following. When I turned to thank the guard, I caught sight of the rude fellow still watching from the sidewalk. I yearned for a downpour of rain or hail, but instead, something delicious happened.

The celebrated Met Opera director Rudolf Bing was just coming out the door as I approached. He lifted his hat and, for whatever reason, greeted me with the warmth of an old acquaintance. "Yes, how've you been, dear Mr. Bing?" I called out, as I slipped into the welcoming dark doorway alone for my backstage visit with a gypsy.

*   *   *

In the morning I was scheduled to take what was called the French train from Cairo down to Aswan, a fourteen-hour ride. I say "down," though direction is reversed there. It's based on the flow of the Nile, so toward Sudan in the south one goes to Upper Egypt, while Cairo in the north is Lower Egypt. Enough geography—this is a wedding story.

I'd no sooner stuck the key in the hotel door when a party of four or five laughing young women ran toward me screaming, "You have to come, you have to come. Come with us!" I told them I'd just drop my suitcase (always travel light) in the room and come along. If they were having that much fun, I didn't want to miss it. As we ran down the hall they explained that a foreigner is needed for good luck at a wedding. Since I had no plans but to read in bed that night, it was good luck for me, too.

The ladies seated me at a table of ten, which quickly absorbed me with geniality (no need to speak of my passport's Israel stamp as point of departure) and the large hall, filled with ten-seat tables, was exuberant. Men and women stood and belly-danced in their Sunday best, while the video cameras rolled, preceded by moving high panels of lights. I'd once studied belly-dancing for six months, but prudence kept me in my seat. The hosts served little food, nuts and cakes, as I recall, and that made me wonder why weddings need to be extravagant when the event itself engenders enough joy and people can go home and eat.

Three invitations to their homes came from families at my table, but I was leaving in the morning. One of my ponderings on the train the next day was what that bride and groom would think years from now when they saw this fair-haired person having the best of times in their keepsake video. Even without belly-dancing.

*   *   *

The train came to a squealing, head-snapping halt, then utter stillness. Gradually my fellow passengers, all Mexicans, began conjecturing to one another. At least two babies started wailing. We were on scrub prairie as flat as a desert in all directions, without a building in sight. Then a loudspeaker in Spanish and static: "The train will not be continuing. There is a highway several hundred meters to the east where you can try to find a ride north to Tijuana." That's where my flight to San Francisco was due to leave in four hours on Western Airlines. These were the days when a missed flight was a total forfeit, and I was teaching at San Francisco State the next day.

Always travel light and wear comfortable shoes, I say. Disgruntled to various degrees, we all descended and started the long trudge over uneven prairie to the road. The other hitchhikers were more fortunate or less picky than I and rapidly found drivers who flung open their passenger-side doors with broad smiles. I turned aside when single drivers passed, there were no single woman drivers, and some cars were packed with families. One of these nevertheless decided there was room for me and my bag, slowed down, and welcomed me in. There were father and mother, Grandma, three little ones, two on laps, and me. My Spanish was adequate but the Señor wanted the children to hear how well he spoke the English he'd learned while working in Los Angeles. He was confident he could get me to the airport in plenty of time, no problem. "No problem," became his mantra.

Before long, one of the children needed to relieve himself, so Papa found a garage and everyone had a soda while one went in to pee. After a quarter-hour, another had to go, and the scene was repeated. I asked Señor timidly more than once whether we could still make the plane in time. Of course, sure, no problem. Then Grandma needed to stop, and I didn't know how to suggest an economy of stops—I just suffered internal nail-biting. At a certain point, glancing at my watch, I had to come to terms with the impossibility. Departure was at one o'clock and it was twelve-thirty. Still, the Señor remained cheery and assuring. I didn't have money for a hotel and pictured sleeping on my handbag on plastic airport seats.

Finally, when we arrived at Tijuana Airport at one-fifteen, an onlooker seeing our farewells at the car would suppose us to be cousins. The Señor accompanied me to the Western Airlines counter. The plane, we learned, would be leaving at two-thirty, and as we shook hands he reminded me with more than a little pride that all Mexicans are nicely relaxed about time.

*   *   *

It's good economics to choose cities with a railway right to the airport. That's the case with Brussels. In the snowy November of 1985 I had to connect with a very early flight, so I found hotel Amigo, only two blocks from the rail station, and had the timetable at hand. Everything was set.

In the morning I got to the station escalator to find it wasn't running. This was dismal news, because the stairway alongside the escalator was the longest I'd seen outside of Russia. I had to haul my suitcase up at least a hundred steps. Taking a deep breath I started up the stairs, and was more than halfway up when I saw the escalator begin to move. What rotten luck, I thought, that they've fixed it now. But it wasn't luck. A man had activated the motor by placing his foot on the bottom step. Ignorance is not necessarily bliss.

*   *   *

I wonder about luck, whether it exists. On a recent trip, hurrying to the Florence train station by bus from the airport, I got engaged in conversation with a couple to my right. I was sitting near the window on the left side, with my red bag wedged between the wall and my thigh. I chose a red bag for easy identification of the precious container of passport, cash in dollars and euros, medication, and cosmetics. If someone were to snatch it, I could shout to the watching world, "Lo sacco rosso! Lo rosso!" My suitcase was stored in the bus's side compartment, and in my rush to get in line to fetch it, and in conversation with my neighbors, I uncharacteristically left the bus without the red bag.

At the station two blocks away, all at once I realized the disaster and ran with the large suitcase back to the bus station, but my bus had taken off. Distraught, I told the dispatcher my tale of woe. The bus had to reach another station and return with other passengers aboard, but he encouraged me to stay calm and wait.

After twenty minutes he beckoned, telephone in hand, to say that a passenger had found the bag and it was on its way back. No doubt looted, I was sure, because I'd carelessly tossed in a handful of bills. But the sweetest kind of shock: everything was there. And the dispatcher declined a tip. I did force on him a mini-bottle of Scotch from the bag. It just seemed right.

*   *   *

How did I get to live with a family in Venice in 1955 for 1,000 lire or $1.50 a day, including meals, laundry, and friendship? A train ride.

The trip from Paris to Milan is one hour now by jet, but

in a slow train at that time it was endless. I had gone up to the map of Europe on the wall of the Paris rail station and closed my eyes and pointed. When I opened them and saw it was Milan, I was disappointed, because it wasn't a new place for me. But the finger had landed.

It was June. I'd just finished the school year in England. Students enjoyed half-price discounts all over Europe, making the third-class fare very low, and conductors inevitably glanced at my ticket and led me to a second-class compartment. This time the conductor, playing father figure, stage manager and Cupid, installed me with two engaging men, traveling separately.

One was a painter from Honfleur, Charles Simon—in French it sounded more romantic, Sharl Seemone—terribly sexy. The other was Pino (Joe) from Rovigo, an innocent, comedic type studying economics at the university in Venice.

During the trip there were many stops, with enough time for each of the men to go out to the platform. They took turns buying beverages and sandwiches, leaving the other to exploit his absence to romance me, one with deep earnest eyes, the other with a twinkle and a joke. Whenever one left, the other stepped up the intensity of his wooing, so that I was asked to accompany Charles to Honfleur, where he would paint, and Pino to Venice, where he knew families that rented rooms to students and had summer vacancies.

My choice became clear. With Charles Simon I would fall wildly in love, forget all sensible plans, get pregnant, become a thick-waisted competent cook, and eventually be dropped like an ash tapped from a cigarette. With Pino I would find other students, develop friendships, learn Italian, have a lot of laughs, and keep my virginity a bit longer. And with my Olivetti portable I would write great one-act plays.

We made our farewells with the handsome painter and transferred to a local train to Venice. We stopped at Rovigo, where I would stay at a hotel while Pino visited his parents overnight. But no Rovigo hotel had any single rooms, until it dawned on Pino that when they saw him they thought I was trying to cheat them. So we went back to the first place, I took a double room, and the clerk was taken aback to see us shake hands and Pino leave. The maid, finding me in the morning sleeping in the soft cot next to the hard bridal-suite bed, scolded me for wasting money. In fact, I'd just spent a good part of my whole summer's allotment, leaving just $100 before the ship left England in late August. Pino thought I could manage it, and I did.

I have thought from time to time of Charles Simon.

*   *   *

When I was small, six or seven at most, my mother took me with her on a train trip to "the south." The black man wearing a red cap, who was called a redcap (and colored, not black), called me "Missy" and his tender voice and look made me feel safe. I'd seen a black man in my first movie, dancing with Shirley Temple. I don't know what state of the Union we were going to—Mother isn't around to tell me—but she had relatives as near across the line as Baltimore. All I remember about the trip was a shock I never came to terms with.

It was hard to find seats, and because we didn't have much luggage Mother took me by the hand to trek through cars filled with rows of people and suitcases, car after car, to search for two seats. I never noticed that all the passengers were white, because our town of 15,000 was all white except for maids. But when we got to one car, it was one-hundred percent filled with black people, old, young and between. I was fascinated but tried not to show it. Then the next car was all white again, and we finally found a pair of seats and never spoke of it. "It" was the question: what would it be like to be sitting there, black, looking at me cloaked in freedom to walk from car to car? I imagined myself being one of them, and this process has never ended.

An echo of that moment happened when I was thirteen, in Atlantic City, where my family stayed at a decent but run-down hotel, the Arlington, near the beach—one of hundreds like it torn down decades later for the casinos. The elevator operator, Ellis, was a handsome young black war veteran. Ellis—that probably wasn't his real name—and I would sit in the open metal elevator cage listening to fight broadcasts, especially of our super-hero, Sugar Ray Robinson. One day Ellis told me his sister was coming up from the south the next day, and he'd have the day off for the beach. When I gushed that I'd look for them, an odd look came to his face, but I ignored it.

The next day I walked alone to the beach, thinking that my friend and his sister would be easy to spot because they'd be darker than the others. When I got there, though, I couldn't find them, and it slowly occurred to me that there weren't any other black people there either. I strolled along among the sun-bathers southward towards Ventnor, and after several blocks came to a sector of beach starting at one street and ending at the next, crammed with only black people. I'd never find Ellis and his sister, and even then I felt such profound shame that I didn't want to face them. I didn't know how to explain the shame to myself. I just knew that, as on that train southward, I was part of something very, very wrong and I wanted to fix it and didn't know how.

Another echo was of Pat Smith, the first "Negro" woman accepted at my undergraduate college. I liked her, and when my roommate left school, I asked to have Pat as my roommate—they had assigned her a single room. The answer, not from Pat but from the Dean, was decidedly no, for the sake of both of us. I felt shame for everyone and still wanted to fix things.

I still don't know how. The Chair of my Department, whose hiring I'd eagerly endorsed, not because he is African-American but because of his expertise, denied me an office to advise students when my course load diminished, and otherwise did much to make my work-life wretched. At one point he candidly expressed resentment against "liberals" who behaved as if blacks couldn't raise themselves up on their own.

Catch 22. But I'm grateful to him now for keeping me from sentimentalizing, keeping the complexity.

*   *   *

John, my first lover, telephoned exactly twenty years after my initiating experience, though of course he had less reason than I to remember that June 16 in New York—it was a coincidence. He suggested we meet in D.C. and take the train to Richmond together for a reunion of sorts. We would meet at Union Station and reserve on a particular train.

I waited until the train was about to pull out and

boarded to take my seat, next to a friendly young sailor in white at the window. It was disappointing but not astonishing, something of a fairy tale anyway, and I was spared seeing that heart-throb grown paunchy and bald. The sailor and I got into a conversation about baseball.

After a few minutes I felt a hand on my shoulder and heard a voice say my name, a voice that still thrilled me to the quick. He had boarded at the end of the train and hunted from car to car. He was not paunchy or bald but looked very much the same. With brief apologies to the nice sailor, I joined John in another seat, to embark on a reprise of a sweet old story. A train can be a friendly place.

*   *   *

I've known few people who were very wealthy. Bill was an heir to a fortune made from dolls, and he lived quietly in Tompkins Cove. He was a shy and sweet roundish person, intelligent but not interesting, and suffered, it seemed, from the same emotional ailment as a college friend of mine. This friend, Ruth, was so certain that men would be interested in her only for the mansion with butler and not herself, that she asked me to set her up on a blind date with the ruse that she lived in my dorm.

I did that, and when the young man didn't call her again, her theory was confirmed. My date explained that his friend simply wasn't interested. So when Ruth next phoned I told her he was transferred out of town without time to explain and sent his greetings.

The parallel came back to me as I rode on the train several successive weekends to the station near Tompkins Cove, where Bill took me to stay with his best friends. He collected me every day and we spent most of the weekends together. He was smitten and I was touched—a classic story we've all been on one side of or the other. When he declared his feelings, I told him that I wasn't in love but that I liked him immensely and he could make love to me. He was dismayed and would not. There was always plenty to reflect on during the ride back to Manhattan. Should I not have gone?

A mutual friend called to tell me a couple of years afterward that Bill had taken his life. My insensitivity couldn't have been the cause, but it's possible that the scenario was repeated until it became unbearable.

*   *   *

Tom, a Czech, worked for Zbigniew Brzezinski at Harvard while I worked on the same Soviet exchange at Columbia. We had lunch in New York a few times, and then he invited me to Cambridge for a weekend.

Tom arranged for me to stay at his apartment while he stayed with a friend—those days seem now to be altogether Victorian. Tom met me at the railroad station with a bouquet of violets, saying it was according to his mother's instructions. He referred to his mother often and was proud of her affair with a noted figure in the British Cabinet. He himself was timid and reticent.

We spent some pleasant time together, exploring Harvard and looking at picture books of Prague in his apartment, and after I left he sent frequent notes of anticipation of our next meeting. Many of these were from other states, particularly California. Then a postcard arrived from Los Angeles. It said that I should forget him entirely, put him out of my mind, and I would never hear from him again. It was easy enough not to think of him, but the drastic tone from someone so mild mannered surprised me.

A decade later I heard Walter Cronkite on CBS News announce that a CIA agent with Tom's name had disappeared and "foul play was suspected." CIA, cloaked in intrigue! Thirty years later, I met Tom's uncle at a folk-dance event in Berkeley and got to see a scrapbook about his nephew's still-enigmatic fate. It turns out that Tom's disappearance caused a dramatic rift between the FBI's J. Edgar Hoover and the CIA.

My favorite memory of Tom remains his story that as a visiting scholar in Leningrad he had showed students in the cafeteria how to cut open a pineapple, one of a batch sent from Fidel Castro. They had no idea how to approach this odd object like a grenade with spiny leaves, or how it might taste, salty or sweet. Like Tom, I enjoyed that story and used it in class. All the rest was unpleasant and sad, hardly what violets at a train station seemed to presage.

*   *   *

Roommates at a conference in Nanjing, Mariko Hori, a scholar from Tokyo, and I were brave enough to travel to Suzou, the Venice of China, though the train information baffled us both. When we had to get back to Shanghai the next day, we couldn't decipher the schedule or even which platform to stand on. We were due back for a meeting and needed help. Secretly—we never spoke of it—I wondered if Chinese recollections of the historic Japanese slaughter of thousands—the Rape of Nanking—would lead people to be rude to my friend. Finally, in desperation she drew characters on a notepad, relying on the similarity which didn't extend to spoken language. We showed the paper to a taxi driver, who responded with great kindness. He took us to the platform facing the right direction, traced the information we needed, worked the notepad, and indicated that he wished us well. That was almost as sweet as discovering Suzou's two-hundred-year-old candy shop.

*   *   *

No conductor ever appeared while I stood for eleven hours in the corridor, suitcase too soft to support me. After Africa, I'd visited a friend in Toulon, in southern France, and had to return to Brussels to catch the plane home. I boarded the train late evening, with a reserved second-class ticket. But when I found the assigned compartment, I faced three completely drunk Danish young men who welcomed me with shouts, loosely flailing arms, and bodies sprawled around like laundry. I couldn't go in. The smell was bad enough, but the prospects were more forbidding, so I waited outside the sliding door for a conductor. After an hour I looked in vain up and down through the cars either for a person to help or a vacancy. At last I sat on the soft luggage with shoes and other hard objects poking and passengers stepping over me. Since then my heart has leaped at the arrival of conductors.

*   *   *

Cuzco in Peru sits at 10,000 feet of altitude, but when you take the ancient zig-zagging train down to Macchu Picchu, the impression is distinctly of ascending. The old train makes a grand effort and you marvel at how it manages every day, with local workers and tourists packed in. On the return up to Cuzco, you feel certain that you are coming down from the mountain. You are also certain that some mishap is immanent, and the guide warned me it could be anything from bandits or the Shining Path guerrillas to a mechanical failure. It turned out to be the second.

A spout of steam, as from an espresso machine, shot up from a radiator very near us, and a crewman came running with a heavy pail of water. He explained there was a hole in the radiator and he would have to keep filling the container throughout the journey, another three hours—there was no way to make repairs and it was too dangerous to stop. Some travelers, not only women, grew rather crazed with fear, but I'd learned to trust old trains. The illusion that we were descending rather than straining to climb eased the suspense. Sometimes it's helpful to fool ourselves.

*   *   *

Standing on the platform next to my little white suitcase, I waited for the train to New York from Philadelphia, where I was in college. A group of friendly young men began circling around me, addressing me by name, so I thought they must be in my cousin's fraternity at the University of Pennsylvania. When they asked me to sit with them on the train, I did, and soon they disclosed that they were the hockey team the New York Rovers. And they said they would like me to be their mascot. (Yes, in the days when employers could grab buttocks with impunity, a woman might not be outraged at such a proposal.) When we parted ways, I asked how they knew my name if they weren't students. Easy, they'd read the tag on my suitcase. That was the last time that ever happened.

*   *   *

While staying with friends in their Vienna home, I took a train to Budapest for a few days. When I got back it was three in the morning, and the snow was very deep. I shook my head awake. The night was utterly silent and clear, my bag was light, and my down coat was still warm from the train. A few flakes still fell.

Exhilarated, I decided to walk the whole distance and found myself in a mood of unaccountable triumph and safety. As my steps broke the snow's new crust, I started to sing out loud, "Who's got the last laugh, who's got the last laugh, who's got the last laugh now?" Here I was, in Hitler's Austria, and he wasn't. On a night like this, it didn't take much to feel giddy.

*   *   *

Last year I took the train to Salinas to visit a man, now in his eighties, I had lived with in the beatnik sixties in Big Sur. He'd been a friend of Henry Miller, had been wounded at Iwo Jima, and was a fine teller of tales. His landlady wrote me that he was slowing down and wanted to see me, and she would meet me at the station.

During the three-hour train ride I was engaged in a war with myself, because he had earlier written to ask me for two thousand dollars to get teeth, like Anse Bundren in *As I Lay Dying*. I could afford it, but somehow I resisted. 1) Am I Santa Claus? 2) Wouldn't anyone like just to ask and receive money? 3) He hadn't been a good lover anyway. 4) Why had he neglected his dental care? 5) We'd only exchanged birthday and Christmas cards for the past three decades. 6) He has a son. 7) He once hit my dog. And so on. But I am a loyal friend, and had helped him out with a few hundred to fix his ancient car. Was I mean-spirited? In any case, I was embarrassed.

It was good to see him. He seemed healthy but had only a few teeth going north and few south. I was hesitant to ask—clearly he hadn't had success.

But he had! He talked about the rich people he'd known in Big Sur who answered the letters of appeal with claims of being broke, but a woman he'd known in high school, widow of a tycoon, sent him a generous amount—and he'd had upper and lower plates made. They were uncomfortable, though, and lay in a box while he used a blender for his meals. When I exclaimed that adjustments, even repeated, could make them fit better, he looked off dismissively into space.

Chatting later about his circulated letters of appeal, he asked, "In your letter, what amount did I write?"

Here he was, not even using the plates, paid for by some kind woman to the rescue, believing she was acting in service to an old acquaintance. And here I was, suffering over not sending one of the various amounts he advertised.

On the train ride home I was visited by a sense of release.

And back on my kitchen counter I wrote a half-dozen substantial checks to people and causes I chose.

*   *   *

I've let down my share of people, but probably none as sorely as Thad Walker, who called and asked me to take the train to Carmel in ten days. That trip didn't end at all in release. Thad was one of hundreds of men I was interested in for something between an hour and a week. In his case it was until he drove his pink Cadillac at twenty miles an hour till I felt like stepping on his accelerator-foot. There was something gentle about him, though, and he liked coming over to talk.

Thad said more than once that talking with me was like reading *The New Yorker,* a more welcome compliment than if he'd said I looked like Grace Kelly. But he was physically involved with Joy, a pot-smoking partner he tried repeatedly to abandon but couldn't quite. Thad had a lovely baritone voice and sang in choral groups—and did some writing, though without intent to publish. And as in the case of most amateur writers, he disclosed more about himself than he meant to. One story—I still have a copy—describes a young man's fastidious preparation to commit suicide. He tidies up his life in exacting detail, from clothing to home furnishings to written records, his car, his kitchen, his friendships. And only when he's satisfied that everything has been entirely put in order is he ready to do himself in, and he does.

I'd taken up with someone else and assumed Thad was still smoking with Joy, when he got in touch some time later. His voice was reduced to a harsh whisper when he called from the Veterans' Hospital in Palo Alto, about to be released to his family home. Part of his shoulder had been excised to use in repairing his throat and vocal cords. He was going to move in with his mother and sister in Carmel. It was important that I visit, so I did.

He was in bed in a sunny garden-facing room, and seemed truly glad to see me. He'd lost much weight and was dying. He had a favor to ask, and he waited to be sure no one could hear. He had me check the hallway. Then he asked it.

"Would you get me a gun?"

"Oh, my God," I responded. "What are you thinking?" Not very perceptive, but a time-filler.

"Look, I can't stand being dependent on them," he nodded toward the rest of the house. "I just can't stand it." We were quiet for a while—it was hard for him to talk and for me to listen.

He said, "I could hide it. No one would know who brought it."

"I can't do that, Thad. They'd know, there are ways of tracing, I'd be in collusion, I'd live with it all my life, it's a selfish request." What I was really feeling, behind this fumbling, was something like Conrad's Kurtz's "The horror. The horror." The horror of feeling as he felt.

His eyes closed, I supposed in resignation. After a few minutes his mother came in, asking if I'd like some tea and nice ginger cookies she'd just baked. Thad winced and inhaled sharply, as if she'd attacked us, then sought my face pointedly as if maybe now I'd reconsider. It was clear he despised every minute trapped in the care of these doting women. I thought then that it may not be the losing of life that terrifies us so much as not having the choice of circumstances.

I've had to say farewell to dying friends before and since, but with Thad I knew he thought I'd failed him, that I'd been the selfish one. I suppose Joy had done so, too. He didn't mention her, but I thought her name and its absence were oddly right.

*   *   *

Once upon a time I stopped a train. Or rather it stopped for me. I was going to work one Saturday from college. I had, in all, seven part-time jobs, one selling handbags on Saturdays in a Philadelphia shoe store, and I was late this morning. The train was pulling out as I ran wheezing and puffing from the underpass to the platform. I must have looked deranged in the engineer's mirror. He stopped with a great noise, then backed up and stopped again just long enough for me to climb on, then started out over again. I have never again felt such a sense of wordless persuasive power.

*   *   *

My talented cousin Sonya was having a premiere in Richmond, Virginia, of an opera she wrote the libretto for. Eager to be there, despite being low on cash, I flew east to Washington, a simple two-hour train ride from Richmond. But it wasn't simple; the train turned out to be entirely full. The only way I could arrive by curtain time was to pay an extra seventy dollars for a sleeper. So I've had the luxury of private bed and bath for all of two hours. I used both towels.

*   *   *

A sobering stop for tourists in the nation's capital is the Holocaust Museum, which draws visitors apparently of all persuasions and ethnicities. The Museum features a cattle-car replicating those that conveyed deportees in Europe to their hideous fates. Visitors are expected to walk through and reflect on what horrors took place. I hesitated at the doorway of the empty car, nauseated by the stench from the imaginary bucket in the corner. Then I decided. No. I refused to enter, on behalf of all those who could not refuse.

*   *   *

After a visit to Budapest, I spent a few more days back in Vienna with my hostess and her newborn, then ventured out again, two hours farther, to Prague.

Again, the snowflakes, again the Soviet soldiers, again the search for a hotel—this time the Intercontinental had a special. With the guidance of a Soviet officer who looked fourteen and wanted to study in the U.S. to be an opera singer, I walked across the whole gently snowy city to the river. The next morning, on a city tour, I found myself standing near an exceptionally handsome young man, perhaps half my age, very tall, in a black leather jacket. He resembled the pre-accident Christopher Reeve. Curiously, I found him standing near me during each stage of the tour, and afterwards he kept pace with me down the long steps and walked alongside, asking if I felt like having lunch. I told him right off that I had only seven dollars. That seemed not to be important, and we lunched together pleasantly. He told me he was from Vienna and that the guesthouse he'd found was a gem, and persuaded me to move there.

The room I took was just below his, and he was right, it was twice as nice for half the price. He took me to the Synagogue and the street where Kafka lived, and as we dined at the guesthouse that evening he showed a flatteringly proprietary attitude towards me.

For some reason, I was gripped by terrific stomach pains, probably inevitable with all the new cuisine. When he invited himself to my room to talk, I was bent over with real pain. The subject he wanted to talk about was the question of whether a man and woman could ever be friends without the sexual element between them. I took one side of the argument, he took the other. I thought it was probably ironic that this gorgeous creature was in a room alone with an older but not too old woman for several hours with nothing sexual happening. I finally asked him to leave me to my misery, and after outlining his plans for us the next day, he said he'd see me at breakfast.

At breakfast I looked around and waited, feeling self-conscious in the group who'd watched us the evening before. I surely looked, turning to scan left and right, like a woman who'd been screwed and dumped. Finally, withered by the staff's knowing eyes bearing down on me, I asked for my companion by name at the reception. "No, madame, he checked out late last night." An old story, I could see in their faces, and wanted to shout, "No! Not this babe!" But he had managed to humiliate me.

Now my Vienna hostess, having delivered her son two weeks before, was ready for something capricious. She dressed me in her sable coat and hat and drove to the station to meet the next train from Prague. She wanted him to see me looking cool, duchess-like, on top of the world. We waited and watched each passenger get off, and he wasn't there. Anyway, she had her outing and her spirits back. And her generous whim eclipsed the put-down.

*   *   *

Kalashnikov rifles and near-bursting bladders are what I remember from the overnight train between Moscow and St. Petersburg, no longer Leningrad. After Peristroika, civil order diminished, and robbers had a field day stopping and holding up trains. In the capital I'd taken up with a charming Venezuelan gentleman in his eighties and his two daughters, and we decided to travel together. The tourist office gave us Stern warnings, along with ordering armed guards to accompany us. One warning, reinforced by rumor, was not by any means to try to use the toilets. While their father slept in his own compartment, the three of us stayed up all night talking about men, never exhausting the subject, not drinking any liquid, and trying for all we were worth to put off peeing until we arrived. One woman passed our compartment holding her nose with one hand and her chest with the other, signaling she was about to faint. So that's how complete strangers came to be dear friends. Trains again had forged my social life. Otherwise the night passed without incident.

*   *   *

In the summer of 1980 Europe sweltered. I'd spent a month in London, where theatre-goers, unaccustomed to a need for air conditioning, suffered without it and mostly went to the parks instead. The notion of traveling south was odious, but I'd promised a friend in a small town near Modena, in the Communist region of Reggio Emilia, that I'd visit in August. She had taught me Italian when I'd lived in Venice a quarter-century before and was tending her father after her mother's death.

The conductor on the train out of London held to custom, even outdid himself, placing me in a first-class compartment. Two elegant silver-haired men, Pavel and John, close old friends, welcomed me. They were proud to be part of the Polish force called The Carpathian Lancers, now without a country and exiled on several continents. Though anti-Fascist, the Lancers were anathema to the Communist regime. They said they'd been among the liberators of a town called Loreto, and their present mission was to place in the town square a plaque—they tapped gently on its wrappings—commemorating the event. The Pope had blessed the plaque, and nothing could ever persuade these two to let it out of their sight until it was properly installed.

Well, something did persuade them. When we crossed from Dover to Calais by ferry, both men became dreadfully seasick, staggered to the rail, and eventually had to go down to the toilet. I was cheerily enjoying the crossing. So they made the decision to trust me with the sacred plaque, which I earnestly vowed to guard with my life.

When that part of the trip had passed and we continued on the train down through Italy, a particular bond grew between us, which they said they would write about in their monthly newsletter. We settled into the train's comforting rhythm, looking out the windows and thinking our thoughts.

The train would continue to the city of Bologna, where

we imagined the weather must be beastly, but we were getting off earlier for our difference missions. After the exchange of warm farewells I was soon on the platform at Modena, my now grey-haired friend running to grab my suitcase.

Her white-mustached father delighted me, in his eighties still cheerily bicycling at sunrise to the bakery for the day's long baguette, his gruff voice holding forth in the kitchen with ardent Communist partisanship. Early evening was balmy and windless—that week the temperature climbed to thirty-nine degrees Centigrade, well over 100. My friend and I left for a bike ride around the village and to survey the famously rich fields—all touted as the product of Communism. But as we started out, the father shouted from the window with all his might. "Come back, come back!" So we did, and he was summoning all the neighbors as well, to stare at the television news. Guerillas had struck again, this time at the Bologna railroad station, where seventy-six people on the train and in the station had been slain and hundreds injured. The photos were numbing. I still have the next day's *Tribune*. The father kept pointing to me, and for days after, as if I were part of some miracle—"This American was on that train! She was on that train!" My own thoughts were that those Polish heroes who detested Communism had been on that train as well, but were now safe and being honored in Loreto, along with their plaque.

They both wrote later and sent a copy of the Carpathian Lancers newsletter with an article about our encounter. It was in Polish, but no matter, I saved it.

*   *   *

Musician friends invited me last year to go with them to the Music Festival at Evian-les-Bains on Lake Geneva, also called Lac Leman. (Evian is the source of the famous mineral water, now owned, according to the ways of the world, by Dannon.) It would be a long train ride with one transfer. Before leaving Paris I stopped at Shakespeare's Bookstore on the Left Bank, where I could count on finding a used paperback to read, in case of rain, while the musicians were rehearsing and doing whatever musicians do to fill the day.

"Hmm," I reflected, coming upon Mary Shelley's classic *Frankenstein* for just three euros, "I somehow never got around to reading this, so now's the time."

The reading went quickly, between bedtime in the usual too-faint light of even pricey European lodgings and cozying by day into the window-seat at the Ermitage Hotel, where I tended to alternate my gaze from page to landscape. The bell-tower, the green slopes, the lake beyond, were more than compelling—they were echoing Shelley's words. When I looked up from descriptions of Mont Blanc and "the amphitheatre of mountains," when the good Dr. F. is finally united with his bride Elizabeth, I was looking at the place Shelley described. I was where the couple in the novel stayed and where the monster slew Elizabeth. Shelley writes, in Chapter 22, "The spire of Evian shone under the woods that surrounded it"—the very scene before me.

And the music performances were splendiferous, predictably, with John Nelson conducting the Ensemble Orchestral de Paris. The featured cellist, Alexander Kniasev, made me weep. I was drunk on life.

*   *   *

Epilogue

A PERSON CAN HAVE an overseas adventure without leaving home. That happened in '56 or '57 in Chapel Hill, when friend Barry Farber was selling ads for a brand-new magazine, *TV Guide*. Barry won a grant to visit the Soviet Union, with a stop at Zagreb, Yugoslavia, where he would be staying at a professor's home.

In Zagreb, the professor's son was another energetic genius the same age and a devout Marxist. I would have enjoyed listening to the dialogue between these two, in view of how in the half-century since then they have honed contrary points of view. Barry is a conservative motivational speaker, talk-show host and writer on how to succeed. He seems to embody the American Dream, a fulfillment of capitalism. The professor's son became himself a professor and prodigious author in several languages on science fiction, the dramas of Bertolt Brecht, philosophy, and the exploring of sophisticated concepts. The two reportedly indulged in lively discourse during Barry's stay, then celebrated at a local student tavern.

Not surprisingly, the subject turned to women, especially American women. The Yugoslav host said he'd met only one, and surmised she wasn't typical. Barry referred by way of example to the last woman he'd been out with. After a few minutes, one of the two (they can't recall which) said my first name. The other found it an odd coincidence, and when they checked on the surname, they rose from the table, shouted to the other students and offered a round of drinks. They all exclaimed over the seventeen million Yugoslavs and more than two hundred million in the U.S.

Barry returned to the U.S. with a souvenir from my very dear old friend Darko Suvin, a record of a folk song. Though the vinyl record broke ages ago, I can today, fifty years later, still hum the whole thing precisely and with immense pleasure. I understand the two men are no longer in contact. I could probably arrange it, but sometimes it's best to let things be, and smile at life's wonders.

About the Author

When not connecting overseas, Marcelline Krafchick, Ph.D., has kept broadly busy in this country, with a base as tenured professor in California for nearly forty years. She's been a board member of Seventh Step, a re-socializing program for ex-felons, president of a homeowners' association, and a radio and television actor. She was the first woman member and chair of the Hayward (California) Zoning Board and Planning Commission, and served on three County and State Commissions. She was the first female professor at Santa Clara University and part of its Honors Program. She authored *World Without Heroes: The Brooklyn Novels of Daniel Fuchs* (Fairleigh-Dickinson University Press) and a section of *O'Neill in China* (Greenwood Press), and co-edited *Speaking of Rhetoric* (Houghton-Mifflin).

She edited *The Carolina Quarterly* and published in *The International Herald Tribune*. She presented academic papers on classical and American culture and literature, and conducted contests for Arts Commission scholarships. She exhibited collected photos of Nepal for two years at California State University, composed questions for Educational Testing Service, renovated a cabin on the Big Sur Coast, and taught modeling both on New York's Park Avenue and locally to Native American women. She cherishes connections with former students in, among other places, Sydney, Louisville, New Orleans, Atami, Mar del Plata, and Budapest, and volunteers at two elementary schools.